TEACHING WITH
COMP ONLINE

An INSTRUCTOR'S MANUAL and
MULTIMEDIA RESOURCE GUIDE

Christine A. Hult

Emeritus, Utah State University

PEARSON

Boston   Columbus   Indianapolis   New York   San Francisco   Upper Saddle River

Amsterdam   Cape Town   Dubai   London   Madrid   Milan   Munich   Paris   Montreal   Toronto

Delhi   Mexico City   São Paulo   Sydney   Hong Kong   Seoul   Singapore   Taipei   Tokyo

Executive Editor: Suzanne Phelps Chambers
Senior Development Editor: Michael Greer
Senior Marketing Manager: Sandra McGuire
Senior Supplements Editor: Donna Campion
Cover and Interior Design: Teresa Ward
Senior Manufacturing Buyer: Roy Pickering

Teaching with Comp Online: An Instructor's Manual and Multimedia Resource Guide to accompany Hult, *Comp Online*

Copyright © 2012, Pearson Education, Inc.

All rights reserved. Printed in the United States of America. Instructors may reproduce portions of this book for classroom use only. All other reproductions are strictly prohibited without prior permission of the publisher, except in the case of brief quotations embodied in critical articles and reviews.

2 3 4 5 6 7 8 9 10–V036–14 13 12

PEARSON
www.pearsonhighered.com

ISBN 10: 0-205-11191-2
ISBN 13: 978-0-205-11191-6

Contents

Part Four: *Research*

Sample Syllabi

Getting Started with *Comp Online*

Comp Online is a new kind of writing guide for composition courses. *Comp Online* thoroughly explains successful writing processes in a way that resonates with a tech-savvy generation. Designed and developed to be used online, *Comp Online* will help your students become more confident and effective writers, regardless of the medium in which they are writing. With over 200 video tutorials, hundreds of writing activities and video-enhanced model documents, and coverage of 20 of the most commonly taught writing projects, *Comp Online* provides students with a complete multimedia learning experience.

The *Comp Online* instructor website is the best place to get started. At the instructor site, you can view a video tutorial to get acquainted with the interface and features of the *Comp Online* etext. You can also learn about using *Comp Online* in tandem with MyCompLab™, download additional instructor resources, and access more information on teaching with technology.

www.pearsonhighered.com/componline

We invite you to access our *Comp Online* demo course to see all that it has to offer. Go to www.mycomplab.com and log in with the login name **componline1** and the password **alwaysteaching1**.

(Note: this account is for reviewing only. You can create a new *Comp Online* course by signing into MyCompLab™ with your own account. If you do not have a MyCompLab™ account, you can register at **www.mycomplab.com** or contact your Pearson sales representative for an access code.)

The book you hold in your hands, *Teaching with Comp Online,* is a printed guide for instructors. In addition to specific suggestions and activities for using *Comp Online*, you will find here general strategies and ideas for teaching writing in an online course environment.

MyCompLab

Comp Online can be used in tandem with MyCompLab™, a flexible application that empowers student writers and teachers by integrating a composing space and assessment tools with multimedia tutorials, services (such as online tutoring) and exercises for writing, grammar, and research.

To learn more, and to view an Online Tour of MyCompLab™, visit **www.mycomplab.com.**

On the MyCompLab™ home page, look for the "How-To Videos and Tours" in the Teaching with MyCompLab™ section. There, you will find video tutorials on registering and creating a course, using the assignment features and the gradebook, using the resources and other instructor features, and more.

The "How-To Videos and Tours" also include a series of video tutorials for students, on topics including reviewing instructor comments on an assignment, using the resources, using the gradebook, and using the composing space.

The *Comp Online* Pre-Built Course

Comp Online is supported by a "pre-built" course in MyCompLab™. This means that the exercises and writing activities in the etext are available for your use in MyCompLab™.

STEP 1: Review the syllabus—You will find the syllabus in the **Course Documents** section of the Home Page. Open the preloaded syllabus, review, and revise as needed.

STEP 2: Make assignments available to students—Click **View Current Assignments** from the **Manage Assignments** section of your Home page. You will find available assignments in the **Current Assignments** and/or **Assignments Requiring Additional setup** folders. Select the assignments that interest you then enter the appropriate dates and adjust the assignment details for each. Be sure to select **Yes** to **Include in List of Active Assignments**.

STEP 3: Hide, show, or assign Resources—Assets in the **Resources** section have been selected to be consistent with the course syllabus. Click **Require/Edit Tutorials and Exercises** from the **Manage Student Resources** section of your Home page to make changes to these Resources.

For more detailed information on managing your prebuilt course, click on the **Help** menu on the MyCompLab™ home page, and follow this path:

Course Management > Create, Copy, or Link to a Course >
Review the Pre-Built Course Materials

If you have any questions about using your prebuilt course, please contact us at **EnglishMyLabs@pearson.com**.

English Instructor Exchange

Professional Development

Valuable for both newcomers and seasoned veterans looking for fresh ideas for teaching as well as grant and publishing opportunities, the hallmarks of this site are the eLectures, podcasts, and video workshops presented by experienced teachers and scholars in composition. As a whole, the eLectures series is aimed at cultivating students' sense of themselves as writers and fostering their abilities to research, draft, collaborate, review and revise effectively; many of the lectures speak to these issues directly. Other topics include writing in the digital age; creating and deploying meaningful and accurate assessments; using ePortfolios and service learning to reach beyond the classroom, and addressing diverse student needs.

From the English Instructor Exchange site, you can also: view archived sessions of *Speaking about Composition*, our online professional development conference series for English; read new and archived editions (as well as submission guidelines) of the peer-reviewed *Open Words* journal; find information about and access to grant opportunities, training resources, technology and media products and Pearson's *Professional Development in Composition* book series; and start or join a conversation about topics of interest to the Composition community.

Visit English Instructor Exchange for practical teaching ideas, instructional support materials, and opportunities to share your own expertise!

www.pearsonhighered.com/englishinstructorexchange

Instructor Resource Center

Getting Registered

To register for the Instructor Resource Center (IRC), go to www.pearsonhighered.com and click "Educators."

1. Click "Catalog & Instructor Resources."

2. Request access to download digital supplements by clicking the "New users, request Access" link.

Follow the provided instructions. Once you have been verified as a valid Pearson instructor, an instructor code will be emailed to you. Please use this code to set up your Pearson login name and password. After you have set up your username and password, proceed to the directions below.

Downloading Resources

1. Go to http://www.pearsonhighered.com/educator, sign in using your Pearson login name and password. Under "Download Resources" search for your book or product by either entering the author's last name or keyword.

Download Resources

Many products in our catalog have instructor resources available for download.
Here's how to access them!

    1. Find your book or product in our catalog.
       Enter the author's last name and a key word from the title:

       [   ] **and** [   ]
       `Go`

---

2. Select your text from the provided results.

    Comp Online
    Hult
    © 2012 | Pearson | Published
    ISBN-10: 0205111912 | ISBN-13: 0205111916

3. After being directed to the catalog page for your text, click the "Instructor Resources" link located under the "Resources" tab.

    Clicking the "Instructor Resources" link will provide a list of all of the book-specific print and digital resources for your text below the main title. Items available for download will have a ⌹ icon.

4. Click on the "Show Downloadable Files" link next to the resource you want to download.

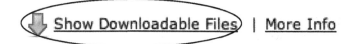

    A pop-up box will appear showing which files you have selected to download. Once you select the files, you will be prompted to login with an Instructor Resource Center login.

5. If you have not already signed in, you will be asked to enter your login name and password, and click the **"Submit"** button.

6. Read the terms and conditions and then click the "I accept, proceed with download" button to begin the download process.

Instructor Resource Center File Download

This work is protected by local and international copyright laws and is provided solely for the use of instructors in teaching their courses and assessing student learning. Dissemination or sale of any part of this work (including on the World Wide Web) will destroy the integrity of the work and is not permitted. The work and materials from this site should never be made available to students except by instructors using the accompanying text in their classes. All recipients of this work are expected to abide by these restrictions and to honor the intended pedagogical purposes and the needs of other instructors who rely on these materials.

Cancel

I accept, proceed with download

7. **"Save"** the supplement file to a folder you can easily find again.

Once you are signed into the IRC, you may continue to download additional resources from our online catalog.

Please "Sign Out" when you are finished.

INTRODUCTION

Get ready to embark on an adventure. I'm very pleased to introduce you to a new kind of writing textbook, one that uses a multimedia online learning environment. With the help of this etext, designed and developed to be explored online, your students will become more confident and effective writers, regardless of the medium in which they are writing. This etext employs well-researched principles of multimedia teaching and learning as developed in the field of instructional technology.

Although the content of this etext will seem relatively familiar to composition teachers, the presentation may not. I've designed this etext to be interactive for the learner. The etext is filled with examples and interactive media to keep the learning active and immediate. Over the years, educational researchers have discovered that multimedia instruction can enhance learning because our brains employ different channels for processing what we see and what we hear. The carefully designed media in this etext, employing both video and audio, will enhance students' learning and accommodate different learning styles.

Throughout the etext, I use an important teaching framework to help students be actively involved in learning the subject matter covered in each chapter. First, I encourage the students to **explore** the information. Exploration takes place through on-screen reading and viewing. Second, I **engage** the students in the material through interactive examples. Engagement takes place through videos, checklists, sample papers, and tutorials. Third, I help the students to **apply** the knowledge gained. Application takes place through numerous *You Try It* practice exercises and writing assignments. This cycle of explore, engage, apply is built into virtually every screen in the etext.

This online etext is a comprehensive resource for college writers that will help your students plan, compose, and revise; do research and formulate arguments; follow appropriate conventions of grammar and style; and write in a variety of genres for various purposes. Students will also learn how to apply principles of visual rhetoric within our increasingly visual world. And throughout, this etext will support students in learning how to use the tools of our new digital environment to their best advantage when composing for academic and future professional success. Best of all, the

1

learning happens through the medium of the Internet, the place where our students "live" many of their waking hours.

As an instructor, you will also appreciate the fundamental emphasis this etext places on both the conventional and rhetorical aspects of good writing, pointing out how even small details should reflect the writer's consideration of audience, persona, genre, field, and writing goals.

Students today use electronic resources to write and format their papers and to gather information. In addition, almost all of them now use social networking tools and sites to communicate—with friends, families, classmates, professors, and the world at large. But often they are unsure about how the conventions of digital communication translate into academic writing. *Comp Online* emphasizes the ways in which the tools offered by this new digital context can assist (or hinder) writers, as well as how to use electronic resources appropriately and ethically.

What distinguishes *Comp Online* from other composition textbooks on the market? It was written as an etext from the very beginning, with consideration of multimedia on-screen learning built into the very fabric of the etext itself. As an experienced teacher of writing, both in traditional and online contexts, I felt the need for an etext that was not originally written as a print publication, but rather began its life online. Each screen was carefully designed to be modular and layered. That is, the information is presented in screen-sized chunks that can easily be digested by the learner. When further information is needed, the learner can delve deeper into the layers of the etext to learn more.

Every screen in this etext is intended to marshal all of a student's learning capabilities through multimedia. The media assets are not add-ons but rather are integral parts of the learning experience. That is, each video, chart, thumbnail, sample document, or *You Try It* exercise moves the learner beyond the flat landscape of a printed text into the multi-faceted landscape of multimedia. The learning principle underlying each screen is "explore, engage, apply." Students are encouraged to first explore a topic, then to engage with the topic through multimedia videos, and finally to apply their learning through *You Try It* exercises and assignments.

How to Use the Instructor's Manual

I wrote this Instructor's Manual to provide you with a wide array of teaching resources for each chapter of the etext—resources that have grown out of my experience teaching writing (in traditional classrooms, computer labs, and online) over a period of more than 25 years, as well as my experiences working with and training new instructors and faculty in various administrative roles, including director of writing, associate department head, and associate dean.

The materials gathered in this manual include multimedia resources, chapter highlights, teaching suggestions, class activities, collaborative activities, computer activities, usage notes, linguistic notes, computer novice notes, ESL notes, connections (cross-references to the etext and to other sources), additional exercises, and *You Try It* exercise answers.

▶ Media Resources

Comp Online is packaged at no additional cost with Pearson's unique and powerful MyCompLab™, which includes a composing and commenting space for students and teachers.

What is MyCompLab™? MyCompLab™ empowers student writers and facilitates writing instruction by uniquely integrating a composing space and assessment tools with market-leading instruction, multimedia tutorials, and exercises for writing, grammar, and research. Students can use MyCompLab™ on their own, benefiting from self-paced diagnostics and a personal study plan that provides the practice students need to improve their writing skills. The composing space and its integrated resources, tools, and services (such as online tutoring) are also available to all students as they write.

MyCompLab™ is an eminently flexible application you can use in ways that best complement your course and teaching style. You can recommend it to students for self-study, set up courses to track student progress, or leverage the power of administrative features to be more effective and save time. The assignment builder and commenting tools, developed specifically for writing instruction, bring you closer to your student writers, make managing assignments and evaluating papers more efficient, and put powerful assessment within reach. Students receive feedback within the context of their own writing, which encourages critical thinking and revision and helps them to develop skills based on their individual needs.

▶ Chapter Highlights

Chapter highlights, which review the key points of each chapter, offer opportunities to orient yourself and your students to the chapter, or to review it for quizzes or before assignments.

▶ Teaching Suggestions

A number of teaching suggestions for each chapter will help you think through your approach to the chapter's content. These suggestions are based on my own experience in teaching writing to various populations at various levels of instruction and in different class settings.

▶ Class Activities

The class activities provide you with fresh ideas about what you might actually do in either a face-to-face class or an online class, and offer reinforcement to the information found in specific sections of the etext. Beginning writing instructors in particular may find these suggestions useful, as they try to decide how best to lead their classes through the material in the etext.

▶ Collaborative Activities

More and more classes include small group work, which can be particularly productive with writing students. The activities here offer some ideas for collaborative or cooperative learning. Collaborative activities can occur either online or in person, depending on the teaching context.

▶ Computer Activities

In addition to class activities, I also provide computer-based activities designed particularly for instructors who teach in computer classrooms or labs. When activities from the traditional classroom can be usefully adapted for computer classrooms (and vice versa), I have noted that additional possibility. For these suggestions, I draw on my extensive experience teaching in a variety of classroom settings, from virtual online classrooms, to networked computer labs, to traditional classrooms with desks and blackboards or whiteboards.

▶ Linguistic Notes

In certain places in this manual, I provide extra information about some linguistic feature mentioned in the book. This might be a historical note about the English language, throwing light on current irregular forms; a discussion of some grammatical or stylistic issue that has been studied in the scholarly literature; or an explanation of some point of linguistic detail about which students (and often others) are frequently confused.

▶ Computer Novice Notes

Although most of our students are now computer literate, some still come into our classrooms with little experience in that realm. The computer novice notes reflect my experience in teaching such students. These notes will alert you to specific problems I have encountered with students who are inexperienced with computers and suggest ways in which you might help these students on an individual basis.

▶ ESL Notes

An increasing number of students are non-native English speakers or members of Generation 1.5—students born in this country but living with families who primarily speak another language and whose oral skills may far outpace their skills as writers of formal English. The etext includes a chapter (Chapter 15) devoted to ESL Issues. To supplement these resources, this Instructor's Manual includes additional ESL Notes aimed at helping instructors understand the problems of ESL students in addition to providing direct instruction to students themselves.

▶ Connections

Connections provide cross-references to related information found elsewhere in the etext itself, as well as references to related articles and books that you may want to locate and read as additional background material.

▶ You Try It Exercise Answers

Answers to the *You Try It* exercises in the etext can be found here in the Instructor's Manual.

▶ Additional Exercises

Finally, this Instructor's Manual also includes ideas for supplementary exercises. In contrast to the Class Activities, the Additional Exercises are intended to be done outside of class. In some cases, however, they call for students to bring materials to class and thus could be turned into traditional classroom activities as well.

How to Use the Media Resources in the Etext

The most exciting feature of this etext is the extensive use of multimedia resources throughout. There are literally hundreds of videos, including several written by students for students, in this etext. To help you use these Media Resources to the fullest, at the beginning of each chapter in this manual, I provide a listing of all the media included within that chapter of the etext.

Using the media resources in a traditional classroom setting. If you typically teach in a traditional classroom, the Media Resources can provide you with unique possibilities for homework assignments. Your students no doubt have access to the Internet, if not on a personal computer, then in a campus lab. By checking the media resources included with each chapter of the etext, you can find appropriate content. For example, if you are teaching Chapter 5.8 on writing effective introductions and conclusions, you might assign your students to view the accompanying videos, which include additional model introductions and conclusions. Having these media resources available will allow you to individualize your instruction to a much greater extent.

Using the media resources in a computer classroom. If you are teaching in a computer classroom or lab, students can begin each class by pulling up MyCompLab™ and working from the resources integrated into the etext, which is included in MyCompLab™. You can help students make the best use of the Media Resources while they are in your class, as well as assign media as homework for additional practice.

Using the media resources with an online classroom. Writing classes are now regularly offered as online courses that lend themselves ideally to the use of media resources. MyCompLab™ and *Comp Online* offer a robust suite of management tools as well as a composing space for your students, diagnostic tools, research resources, and much more. You can set up, share, and grade writing assignments at the same time that your students use *Comp Online* and MyCompLab™ as their basic learning environment.

A Brief Guide to Teaching Composition Online

This brief guide is intended to provide basic strategies and tips for composition instructors who may be new to online teaching. Much of the advice will be directed toward entirely online classes, though many of the general ideas apply equally well to hybrid classes (face-to-face classes with a significant online component). The style and use of online classrooms can vary widely—from a traditional face-to-face class with readings posted online to an entirely online multimedia interactive class experience—but similar principles apply. The overall goal you should be working toward is to find a balance between a rich, valid, and engaging experience for students and a manageable, useable, and expressively viable experience for yourself as an instructor. Driving yourself crazy (which is definitely easy to do when teaching an online course) for the sake of the student experience doesn't create a successful course, and yet keeping things simple for yourself at the expense of the student experience is clearly also a problem.

As you would with any piece of writing, give yourself time to run through several drafts when designing an online class; there's no need to get it perfect the first time, and you'll be tweaking and revising continually even after the semester has begun. Embracing the idea that, just like a face-to-face class, an online class isn't a static, unchanging environment is the first step to successful course design and management.

1. Overview: What Changes When a Course Moves Online?

Most instructors have a comfortable, familiar image in their minds of a traditional college classroom, and the removal of this shared setting alone can be enough to cause panic. It's very easy to tie ideas about how a class works to the setting in which it usually takes place, but rest assured that when a class moves online, not *everything* changes. Many aspects of the teaching experience remain familiar—some are even enhanced by the online environment—and some of what remains familiar may surprise you.

Just as in a traditional classroom setting, online composition classes bring together a community of students who will make their way through the subject together over the course of a semester. The class will involve a variety of diverse assignments, including discussions, workshops, peer reviews, and informal and formal writing. Many instructors who are new to online classes assume that the more interactive aspects of a traditional classroom are eliminated in an online setting, but today's course management programs have gone a long way toward enabling most of the common interactive situations that a composition class calls for. You'll be able to lecture to your students, discuss and workshop their writing, engage in critical readings and peer reviews, and carry on group discussion. The way in which you find yourself *preparing* and *managing* these aspects of your class may change, but the fact that many of your favorite assignments and teaching techniques can cross over into the virtual classroom should be a comforting thought.

Of course, while the basic elements of the class can stay relatively familiar, there are other elements of the teaching experience that are decidedly different when a course moves online, and knowing what to expect can help you prepare to adapt your teaching style accordingly. Three main elements of your class will be unique to an online environment: the pacing, the mode of interaction, and the structure and delivery of information.

Pacing

Most online classes are asynchronous, meaning that the instructor and students are not all online together at a predetermined time. This helps make online classes viable for students who work full time or who are balancing families and schooling; they can log on whenever is convenient for them and complete the course work on their own schedule.

Keep in mind, too, that some students who sign up for online classes do so because they mistake a *flexible* class schedule for a *lighter* class schedule. It's important to warn your students from the start that an online class isn't necessarily going to be any less work than a face-to-face class!

Unless the class is a hybrid, where students are meeting in a physical classroom for a portion of the time, an asynchronous class environment means that your students may never interact in "real time." This is okay—part of adjusting to an online class is getting used to the more drawn-out pace of threaded discussions. Planning your weekly deadlines on a very general timeline (requiring students to log in two times a week—once before Wednesday and once after, for example—as opposed to requiring them to log in specifically on Tuesdays and Thursdays) offers students flexibility, while still allowing for back-and-forth discussions. Arranging for drafts to be posted early at the start of the week, peer reviews to be conducted mid-week, and discussion of the peer reviews to take place at the end of the week allows a decidedly interactive assignment to take place flexibly, outside of synchronized interaction. Also, allowing pairs or small groups of students to arrange their own real-time chats (and making sure the necessary areas of the online classroom are available to them to do so) can take the burden of large-scale schedule coordination off of your shoulders.

Mode of Interaction

Your class's pacing will largely determine the ways in which you interact with your students and they interact with each other. Ideally, your course management system will offer you (and thus your students) a variety of ways to interact: real-time chat rooms, asynchronous forums, email, formal lecture space, and so on. Whereas in a traditional classroom you can move from formal lecture to informal discussion to casual group work with a simple change in tone or a few directions to the class, in an online class, these different modes of interaction are typically designated by different locations in the virtual classroom. For example, formal lecture may take place in the learning module area, while informal discussions take place in the forums. You may choose to set aside private forums for group work, or even a general, fun forum for the sharing of non-course-related materials. Finding ways to incorporate (and organize) a wealth of interactive modes is key to an online class that goes beyond the basic correspondence course model.

For example, imagine you are introducing a new genre to students in preparation for a formal writing assignment. After having them read and watch the videos in the relevant chapter from Part Two of *Comp Online*, you might want to post a formal lecture, screencast, or slide presentation along with an additional example or two of the genre in the learning module area of the class website. You could then pose a discussion question or two about one of the examples on the discussion board, prompting students to read, analyze, and respond to the example through their formal postings to the discussion thread for that topic. To that, you could add an informal chat room or discussion space to allow students to pose general questions about the assignment to each other and to you. Many online instructors have found that a "layered" approach, using both formal and informal modes of interaction in connection with each topic or unit, works well. Providing multiple modes of interaction allows students with different confidence levels and varied learning styles to participate and engage material in ways that make sense to them.

Structure and Delivery of Information

Along with the pacing of assignments, you will need to decide what assignments to deliver and how to use your online classroom to deliver them. Model Syllabi are included in the Appendix of this Instructor's Manual to give you some ideas of where you might begin. If you are using the pre-built *Comp Online* course found in MyCompLab™, the *You Try It* exercises and assignments will already reside in the online classroom space. If you are not using MyCompLab™, check your course management program to see how they suggest posting assignments. Most course management programs these days offer a wide range of options for assignment delivery and assessment. You can keep it simple by having most work posted in a shared space such as discussion forums or emailed to you personally by your students. You can also take advantage of the more enhanced aspects of online classrooms such as plagiarism-detecting programs (if your school subscribes to one) and built-in grading rubrics by having students submit work through a homework manager. And, of course, you'll also need to decide where in your online classroom you're going to put the various other documents and pieces of information, such as the class syllabus and course guidelines, that you'll be giving your students.

Unlike in a face-to-face class, where information is delivered and discussed in diverse formats (syllabi printed and handed out, lectures delivered orally, printed articles taken home to read, desks pulled together for group work), all of the varied work that your students will be doing for their online class will be done in a very similar physical setting: at their computers. This does not mean, however, that there is only one mode of communication in an online class (this will be discussed further later on), but it does mean that the majority of the information that you give your students will be text on a screen. It's up to you to structure that text purposefully and clearly so that assignments, lectures, and readings are all easily located by students.

2. Planning and Organizing an Online Course

View your course through your students' eyes

When setting up your online composition classroom, you have to try to see things the way your students are seeing them. If you're teaching an entirely online course, where your students will never meet you nor each other in person, you need to be aware that your perception of the class—as a semester-long, purposefully-designed entity populated with 20 or so students—is not what your students perceive. As far as they know, they are interacting with the online space in a solitary, isolated manner. This will change as they learn how the class works and how they'll be interacting with you and with their peers, but at the start, you need to keep their initial experience in mind.

Rather than assuming that your online classroom speaks for itself, you want to use the course management tools at your disposal to ensure the class speaks *for you* and *to your students* in a useful way. Imagine yourself walking into a physical classroom full of students and greeting them for the first time. You wouldn't simply launch into the first week's material without saying hello; you'd take the time to introduce yourself, introduce the course, and set the tone for the semester. Greeting your students and orienting them to the course should happen in an online setting, too. There are two levels of information that should be readily available to students from their initial log-in: background information and metered information.

Understand the differences between background and metered information

Background information is made up of static materials that are available from the beginning of the semester and that stay the same throughout, things that can be delivered once and remain applicable for the duration of the class. This includes documents like the class syllabus, the calendar of due dates, your contact information, basic information about how the class works, and the like.

Metered information is the stuff that gets delivered in segments, parceled out as the weeks go by, and that builds upon itself as time passes. This includes things like daily or weekly assignments, lectures, discussion prompts and forums, weekly readings, and so forth.

There needs to be a clear distinction between one-time delivery information and ongoing-delivery information because students will need to know what information is static and what information they will need to check in for regularly. There should be a clearly marked, central "begin here" place that gives students all the background information they'll need and that also includes information about where to go during each subsequent log-in for the metered information.

Use repetition and redundancy to help students focus

An important thing to remember when setting up this basic structure for the class is that redundancy is good, but scatter isn't. This is where seeing things from your students' perspective is important. Imagine this: you send out an orientation email to your students with information about how the class works, and you also create a "begin here" link in the classroom with the same information, because you can't be sure which inroad any given student will apprehend first. This redundancy is good—students have double the chances to get the information they need.

But that double-pronged approach also risks scatter. One of the most stressful experiences online students report is not being sure they're finding all the information they need or that the class offers. So for a student who both receives the email *and* follows the "begin here" link, you want to make sure that you state in each place that the information is the same as in the other. Consider including a line like, "If you received my welcome email then you already know this..." or "if you've visited the classroom already then you probably noticed the 'begin here' link."

Students are surprisingly not bothered by repetition, as long as it's *clearly labeled* as repetition; they're usually relieved to have it confirmed that they're getting the same information twice rather than getting additional, possibly different information. The importance of repetition is also true for tips and guidelines that you want students to be remembering throughout the semester (for example, reminders to post any questions they have to a general Q&A forum, or to log into a chat program to "visit you" during your office hours, or to not put off their interview for the final paper). Go ahead and preface it with "I'm sure you're sick of hearing me say it by now, but..."; what matters is that you get your reminders across on a regular basis and in a variety of locations (in lectures, in assignment descriptions, in announcements, etc.). And within the classroom in general, as many repeated cues as can be given about where the central core of information is located are good—you want to funnel the students' attention to that essential hub.

Design to support nonlinear students

Today's students like to explore. In fact, learning by doing (rather than by reading through a manual first) is touted as one of the defining characteristics of digital natives, which many college students are. It's easier than you'd expect for a student to bypass a link called "course content" or "learning modules" in favor of another link that, for whatever reason, they perceive to be "first" on the webpage. If students stumble upon a discussion forum that has an assignment for them to do during the first week of class, they may assume that they've done their work for the week and log off, completely missing the fact that there were also readings and lectures posted. This actually happened to a well-meaning student in an online class.

While it's true that most students will explore further than the first link they find, it's important to remember that any given student will not move through the online classroom in the same way you would. Especially during the first few weeks of class, *all available links* should redirect students' attention to the place you want them to visit first. Remember, your students are here "alone,"—they can't glance to the side to see what the rest of the class is doing. Making up for that initial lack of social cues is an important design consideration; the classroom has to provide the guidance itself.

3. Building Community

It is a common perception that technologically mediated interaction (as in an online class) is somehow impoverished, that it can't be as socially or emotionally effective or meaningful as face-to-face interaction. The phenomenon known as "flaming"—excessively nasty and aggressive comments made online—is often attributed to this. In online settings, people will sometimes be excessively critical, put forward extreme opinions, and use language that they would never use in a face-to-face social context. It can be hard for some people to imagine this taking place in an online classroom, but as many of the same characteristics are present in an online class as in typical Web forums—anonymity, asynchronous interaction, perceived distance—it can definitely happen. While it is undeniable that some communicative depth is lost through mediation (facial expression, posture, tone, and so on, are hard to determine through typed language, for example), there's no reason to assume that the interaction of an online class is simply relegated to impersonal missives or aggressive attacks.

For composition classes, where a sense of community among students is often an important aspect of the learning environment, the ability to create meaningful social interaction is especially important. Luckily, online space is now recognized as a setting for a vast amount of meaningful interactions; people are finding ways to create a sense of social presence in online settings.

The use of rich media is one such way. Audio and video technologies bring many of the social cues that are lost in a text-only space, and the good thing is that they don't need to be the dominant form of communication. One of the ways that people can maintain meaningful interactions online is because it is instinctive for people to bring their preexisting knowledge of each other to a mediated setting. When people talk on the phone to someone they know well, they can picture the other person's expressions or postures even though they can't see them at that moment. When friends and family members communicate online, via email or in chat rooms, they can imagine each other's tone and picture each other's expressions based on prior knowledge and previous face-to-face experience. Remembered moments of rich interaction make the participants more "present" for each other during times of mediated interaction.

This can be achieved in an online classroom with even the most minimal use of rich media. A brief exposure to your voice, your image, your personality, can give your students a real person to envision when they read your lectures, posts, or emails. They can then overlay their knowledge of your personality onto the less expressive communications they receive from you.

Considering this, it is especially important to let your genuine voice and personality come through. Your goal with the use of rich media in an online class isn't to present a professional training video; it's to introduce yourself as a human being. This is even more important in the more textual instances of interaction. Remember that when you teach face-to-face, you don't have only one voice or one mode of interaction. You move between formal lecturing, casual discussion, and even friendly non-course-related chat before and after class.

These are the multi-dimensional interactive scenarios where online classes typically fail. The use of rich-media isn't enough here, because rich media moments (outside of a fully synchronous, webcast class) aren't interactive. You can present yourself to your students in a prerecorded video, but you can't react to them or see their reactions to you. Thus it becomes important to embrace the use of different voices in different online class situations— you must recognize that just like a physical classroom, the online classroom does not necessitate a single mode of interaction.

While your communication style might be formal and proper in lectures and professional in emails, try to be casual and accessible in discussion forums or chat rooms. You don't need to try to mimic chat or text slang, but do let yourself write more casually. Many instructors worry that informal writing (especially the use of slang and emoticons) simply encourages students to write sloppily, but this is no more true than the claim that friendly chatting before class leads to poorly written essays. Model for your students the point made frequently in *Comp Online* that different styles of communication are appropriate to different venues. Learn to embrace casual typed communication as "expressively useful" rather than as juvenile or careless, and make an effort to draw out students who may think that online interaction means typing only terse, brief comments.

On a similar note, it's important to provide your online students with a forum for casual interaction. While most discussion forums will be designated for assignments, peer reviews, and workshops, keep a forum open for the general posting of questions, ideas, and even fun links, and then model the type of interaction you expect from your students by posting fun, interesting, or thoughtful things there yourself. You can also set up a class Facebook page, or a class Twitter account, or a class blog; not only do these provide fun social opportunities for students to engage with you and with each other in a familiar, casual setting, but they provide opportunities for students to practice writing in different modes. One important caveat to remember here is to make the distinction between required course participation and optional course participation clear. Students shouldn't have to wonder whether posting to the class blog is a graded writing assignment or just an optional fun way to engage with the material.

4. Writing assignments.

Good Prompts for Online Writing Students

One of the benefits of teaching composition online is that there is a wealth of information, inspiration, and provocation continuously at the tips of your students' fingers. While traditional writing prompts will certainly be successful in an online class, consider taking advantage of the opportunities that the virtual classroom setting offers. Building hyperlinks directly into assignment descriptions or instructions is a great way to get your students exploring and thinking their way around the Web. This is an important aspect of an online class, as many students who use the Web as a resource have not yet been asked to think critically about much of its content.

A good starting place when creating many different types of writing assignments is Wikipedia. For example, Video 3.3 introduces students to the idea of using Wikipedia to generate topic ideas. Most students have used Wikipedia as a research tool (as have many instructors), and yet some don't know that it is a collaboratively built encyclopedia that anyone—expert or not—can edit. Many universities and individual instructors have banned Wikipedia as a source in academic writing, but conversely, many academics also admit that Wikipedia is usually more up-to-date than traditional print sources. Students can be asked to consider the topic of Wikipedia from a variety of perspectives:

- **Investigation**: What is Wikipedia? How and when was it created, and for what purpose? What current controversies exist about it?

- **Expression**: Create or revise a Wikipedia entry for yourself, your family, another group of which you are a part, or a subject that you are familiar with. Consider what information belongs in a Wikipedia entry and what doesn't. Consider how best to present the information you deem necessary.

- **Interpretation/Analysis**: Consider the Five Pillars of Wikipedia. Do you feel that these guiding principles are in accordance with each other, or do they contradict each other? If you were in charge, what would you add or alter, and why?

- **Persuasion**: Do you believe that Wikipedia should be an allowable source in academic writing? Why or why not? Support your opinion with examples from the Wikipedia site.

Other topics to which the Internet lends itself are visual rhetoric, netiquette, and amateur news reporting. These are all subjects that benefit from the ease of hyperlinked exploration and that engage students in a way that is both familiar and challenging at once.

Responding to Student Writing

Your online classroom will provide you with various venues for responding to your students' work, both publically and privately. It's important to remember from the start that no discussion of grades should take place in a public forum, as it risks breaking the rules of the Family Educational Rights and Privacy Act (FERPA). Legality aside, however, it can still be a tough decision to know how to balance praise and criticism in a public grading forum, where students stand to benefit from viewing the feedback their peers have received. Just as in a traditional classroom, students certainly appreciate instructors who cheer on their efforts, so make sure that you include positive feedback as well as constructive criticism. Target individual students for praise, highlighting what they did successfully and then offering class-level suggestions and corrections is one way to avoid having an individual student feel singled out as an example of what *not* to do. You can even create hypothetical incorrect examples (perhaps modeled on some specific ones you noticed in the class), as a way of delivering group advice.

Of course, there will be students who do very poorly on an assignment or who otherwise need obvious and straightforward correction or criticism. In these instances, you need to be especially conscious of how easy it can be to deliver criticism when you don't have to look a student in the eye (and keep in mind that your style of commentary is going to provide a model for your students' feedback to each other, and you always want to avoid potential flaming). Visualize how you would address a student's writing if that student were in your office, or in a classroom surrounded by his or her peers. It can be easy to forget that your computer screen houses a "public" space when you work in your online classroom, but it's important to maintain appropriate public versus private feedback. Save directed criticism for one-on-one feedback via email, private chat, or gradebook comments, and keep public comments either specifically or generally positive, or generally critical.

5. Moderating and Motivating: Managing an Online Course

One of the most difficult parts of teaching an online class is managing your time so that you stay on top of your classroom activity without having to be tied to your computer 24/7. In a face-to-face classroom, group discussions allow for the students who have thoughts, responses, or comments to voice their ideas so that you and the entire class can hear them. As an instructor, this is a nice time to let the students carry the class period—as they engage with the topic at hand, you can take the role of director rather than speaker, pointing to the next raised hand, or breaking in briefly to fill in information, guide a subject, or correct a misunderstanding. In an online class, the instructor's role in a discussion is very different.

In an asynchronous online classroom, group discussions take time, and maintaining a presence in a discussion can be incredibly time consuming for an instructor. Students won't get to see your nods and gestures during a group discussion or workshop; they won't know you're "present" at all unless you actually type something. Of course, typing a response to each and every student takes a lot longer than nodding or briefly replying during a face-to-face class. One of the benefits of an online class is that students who wouldn't normally speak up in a group discussion have the chance to contribute; the downside of this greater participation is time spent making those students feel acknowledged.

Embrace brief individual replies, and save longer, extended commentaries for posts to a group or to the class as a whole, or for when a student reaches out to you via email with a specific question. Singling out the posts of one or two students each week as good examples to their classmates is also a good strategy. You can keep a separate column in your gradebook to check off which students have received public praise, so that you can make sure it's distributed fairly.

The use of multiple voices, as discussed above, can help you here, too—it's easy to fall into the familiar academic pattern of written communication being long-winded and formal, but in less formal scenarios feel free to write more briefly and casually. Enthusiastic and appreciative individual responses like "How cool!" or "That sounds great!" not only indicate social presence, but also make a student feel as though her work is being appreciated, while your more substantive suggestions and responses can be addressed to the class as a whole.

As important as it is to avoid burnout by being too involved, however, it is also important to make sure your students feel that you are indeed present in the class. Many online students have reported that truly awful things can happen in a discussion forum that isn't consistently moderated by an instructor. Minor insults and slight (even unintended) personal criticisms that go unacknowledged or unchecked by an authority figure can open the door for increasingly aggressive and inflammatory personal attacks. In an online class, especially a composition class where students' opinions, experiences, and beliefs are often the topic at hand, you simply *must read every discussion post*. You don't need to respond to each, but it is your job to read them and nip any instances of flaming in the bud. The occasional friendly interjection or comment lets students know you're reading what they write, and swift and firm reactions to inappropriate posts send a clear message about appropriate interaction.

It is also imperative that you reply to emails and direct questions from the class in a timely manner. When students feel that their instructors are not listening to their questions or concerns, especially when a student has made an effort to contact you directly, the lack of a timely response communicates to the student that the course isn't important to you. Absent professors are one of the biggest complaints about online classes; just because you've set up a comprehensive and self-explanatory classroom doesn't mean that your students won't still need individual attention and consideration. Setting up a nuts-and-bolts discussion forum for students to post procedural questions is one way to cut down on individual emails, which may all be asking the same question.

The need for a balance is clear: you don't want to overextend yourself, but you don't want to let your class and classroom get away from you. Create a schedule for yourself as well as for your students. Some instructors choose to set aside certain days of the week for administrative work (course prep, lesson planning, and online classroom management) and dedicate other days to more active teaching tasks (forum monitoring, commenting, and grading). Some instructors prefer to balance several days a week with a bit of each kind of work, prepping future lessons in the morning and interacting with students in the afternoon. Whether you decide to check in on your classroom for a short time each day or for an extended time a few days a week, make sure the schedule allows enough time for you to take in all the participation, but keeps your time commitment at a reasonable level. Consider how much time you would normally dedicate to a face-to-face class—in-class time, office hours and student conferences, and course prep time—and plan to, at the least, match that with an online course. If you're designing a completely new class, the time commitment may be much more; not only do you need to prepare lesson plans and actively teach, but you'll need to factor in designing and organizing the virtual classroom in a way that a face-to-face class doesn't require. But don't be afraid to set boundaries on your time--I don't answer student emails on the weekend, for example, and I let my students know this boundary from the outset.

6. Resources and Tools

For additional professional development resources for online teachers and other current topics in the teaching of writing, visit the Pearson Composition Professional Development site at *www.pearsoncomppro.com*.

Among the many books about teaching online, here are two of the most helpful for teachers of composition:

Scott Warnock, *Teaching Writing Online: How and Why* (Urbana: NCTE, 2009)

Rena M. Palloff and Keith Pratt, *Building Online Learning Communities: Effective Strategies for the Virtual Classroom* (San Francisco: Jossey-Bass, 2007)

PART**ONE**

Writing

Chapter 1 /*Saying What You Mean to Say in a Digital World*

Multimedia for Chapter 1

VIDEO TUTORIALS	SAMPLE DOCUMENTS	WRITING ACTIVITIES
Video 1.1 Chapter Introduction	Sample Image Facebook Post	*You Try It* 1.1 Different Kinds of Writing
Video 1.2 Informative Website	Sample Image Email	*You Try It* 1.2 Using the Rhetorical Triangle
Video 1.3 Engineering Report	Sample Image Blog Post	*You Try It*: 1.3 Considering Rhetorical Situations
Video 1.4 Photo Blog	Sample Image Style Sheet	
Video 1.5 Volunteer Request		
Video 1.6: Knowing Your Audience		

Video 1.7 The Evolution of Newspapers		
Video 1.8 The Changing Nature of Writing		

Chapter Highlights

This chapter stresses the important relationship between technology and writing—a topic that recurs throughout the etext. In addition to discussing the ways writing and technology are inextricably linked, the chapter also serves as an introduction to the reasons people write: to communicate, to learn, to create, and to persuade. Once students have thought about why, how, what, where, when, and to whom or for whom they write, they are encouraged to think about how technology affects their writing, as well as to consider the various tools, media, and genres used by writers today. The chapter also helps students consider how writing affects their own lives and understand the profound ways in which technology has altered, and is altering, the communication landscape.

Learning Outcomes

The learning outcomes for Chapter 1 are listed in the following chart, along with the relevant sections of the chapter and exercises that teachers can use to evaluate their students' mastery of the objectives. This chart also appears as a clickable link in the etext.

CHAPTER 1 LEARNING OUTCOMES CHART	
To assess your understanding of the Chapter 1 learning outcomes, work the corresponding You Try It exercises and study the relevant chapter sections.	
1.1 Identify different purposes for writing.	*You Try It*: 1.1 Different Kinds of Writing

1.2 Communicate effectively with different audiences using a variety of media.	*You Try It*: 1.2 Using the Rhetorical Triangle *You Try It*: 1.3 Considering Rhetorical Situations
1.3 Explain the value of writing skills in college and workplace settings.	Study Chapter 1.4b
1.4 Describe the ways technology can be used in the writing process.	Study Chapter 1.4c

Teaching Suggestions

Use this chapter as an opportunity to begin a discussion (either in person or online) with students about their experiences with new information technologies. How many of them use email, text messaging, or social networks, for example? For what purposes? How many of them have a blog or participate in Internet forums like Twitter.com or Facebook.com? How does technology affect their own writing practices and processes?

One of the dangers of the information age is that consumers get in the habit of accepting new technologies unexamined. It is important that thoughtful critiques of the technologies that affect writers be an ongoing part of the agenda in writing classrooms.

Those of you teaching in a computer lab will quickly discover that Murphy's Law frequently applies: whatever can go wrong, will. It is difficult, if not impossible, to foresee the technical glitches that may occur while class is in session. So, just to be on the safe side, you should always have a pen-and-paper activity ready to go at the first sign of technical trouble. In this way, you will ensure that class time is productive, with or without the help of computers. It is also important to have a technical-support person available to deal with those inevitable glitches. You should be able to concentrate on your role as the class's instructor rather than trying to double as the computer technician. Keep your sense of humor and do not take personally anything the computers send your way. Their importance as a writing tool far outweighs any transitory technical problems.

Those of you teaching online will want to have backup plans for your lessons. You can use the telephone or an Internet audio service like Skype to connect with your students if your classroom is down for a period of time. Set up alternative ways to communicate, such as email lists or Google groups, and let students know what the back-up systems will be. The main thing is to keep several channels of communication open so that you don't lose touch with your students for any extended period of time.

1.1 Why do we write?

Class Activities

The following quotations reflect variations on the idea that we write what we know in order to know what we think. Considering that the purpose of writing falls into a few basic categories—to communicate, to learn, to be creative, and to persuade—use these quotations as a springboard for class discussions (online or in person).

> The little girl had the making of a poet in her who, being told to be sure of her meaning before she spoke, said: "How can I know what I think until I see what I say?"
>
> —Graham Wallas, *The Art of Thought*

> That old lady in the anecdote who was accused by her nieces of being illogical [exclaimed,] "Logic! Good gracious! What rubbish! . . . How can I tell what I think till I see what I say?"
>
> —E. M. Forster, *Aspects of the Novel*

> I write entirely to find out what I'm thinking, what I'm looking at, what I see and what it means. What I want and what I fear.
>
> —Joan Didion, *Why I Write*

> No surprise for the writer, no surprise for the reader. For me the initial delight is the surprise of remembering something I didn't know I knew.
>
> —Robert Frost, *The Figure a Poem Makes*

Author note: My thanks to the members of the Writing Program Administration (WPA) listserv for pointing out these quotations to me.

Collaborative Activities

Have students gather in small groups (or online forums) to share their writing logs from *You Try It* 1.1. Ask each group to categorize the types of writing done by its members and to report the findings to the class.

Computer Activities

Have students share their writing logs from *You Try It* 1.1 by emailing them to a classmate or by posting them to an online class bulletin board.

1.2 How important is writing to your success?

Class Activities

Because the ability to write well will get students good grades in school as well promotions in their future careers, it is wise to illustrate to students that reality. To help do so, you might have students consider their past employment or that of their family members. Query students about the writing that happens in those workplaces. Students who instant message, email, or text message should also be aware of technology's influence on writing. Have students project the uses of those technologies into the workplace. This discussion can take place online or in class.

1.3 How do we communicate effectively?

Collaborative Activities

Have students gather in small groups to share their lists from *You Try It* 1.2. Give each group a dry-erase marker and a transparency sheet on which to record a composite list. Share the lists with the entire class using an overhead projector. Discuss similarities and differences between the groups' lists. Try to arrive at a consensus about how various technologies affect students' writing. Online teachers can use a document-sharing space or forum.

Students can work in groups to discuss the writing from the previous activity from a rhetorical perspective. Have them identify the audience, purpose, and persona for their different types of writing by considering the appeals in the rhetorical triangle. You can then have groups share their discussions. This activity can be done in class or in an online discussion forum.

1.4 How does technology make a difference to our writing?

Computer Activities

Use an online chat (synchronous discussion) room for this activity. Have students join separate chat rooms in groups of four or five, as having an entire class in one chat room will slow down the discussion. Ask students to chat online about the ways in which they think technology has altered the communication landscape. After ten or fifteen minutes, bring students back together as a class to share their ideas—in person or in a discussion forum. If you are in a computer lab, to prevent students from being distracted during the discussion by what appears on their computer screens, ask them to dim their monitors during class discussion time. Before leaving the chat rooms, you might even have students examine how that writing differs from, for example, a student essay. Students may want to archive the chat for future reference.

Computer Novice Notes

As you begin to discuss the uses of technology in writing, be aware that students will have varying levels of experience and expertise. Reassure those students who are relatively new to using online media that you will provide them with additional help until they become confident and competent. Also, encourage students who are experienced with various technologies to act as peer tutors for the novices. If you are teaching in a computer classroom, try to situate the experts around the room, and invite them to share their knowledge with the others in the class. Remind the experienced students to be patient with the novices, and acknowledge the help of the experts whenever possible. If you are teaching online, create peer pairs that include a novice and an expert.

Connections

For an interesting discussion of how computer networks change both teaching and learning, see Joan Tornow, *Link/Age: Composing in the Online Classroom* (Logan: Utah State UP, 1997). See also Elizabeth Klem and Charles Moran, "Computers and Instructional Strategies in the Teaching of Writing," *The Allyn & Bacon Sourcebook for College Writing Teachers,* ed. James C. McDonald (Boston: Allyn & Bacon, 1996) and Takayoshi and Huot, eds, "Teaching Writing with Computers: An Introduction" (Boston, Houghton Mifflin, 2003).

Additional Exercises

Share with the class a brief essay on some technology topic. You can share the essay either as a photocopy or as a computer file posted to a network or linked to a class website. Have the students read and discuss the essay, either in person or in an online discussion forum.

1.5 How can this etext help you succeed as a writer?

Answers for Chapter 1 *You Try It* Exercises

For all exercises in this chapter, answers will vary.

Chapter 2 / *Critical Reading and Viewing*

MULTIMEDIA FOR CHAPTER 2

Video Tutorials	Sample Documents	Writing Activities
Video 2.1 Chapter Introduction	Sample Paper Synthesis Essay	*You Try It* 2.1 Critical Analysis of a Purchase
Video 2.2 Establishing Your Purpose	Sample Paper Abstract	*You Try It* 2.2 Analyzing Audience and Purpose
Video 2.3 Synthesizing Information	Sample Paper Headings and Captions	*You Try It* 2.3 Inferences
Video 2.4 A Synthesis Paper	Sample Paper Detail	*You Try It* 2.4 Annotating a Paragraph
Video 2.5 Annotating a Text	Sample Discussion Forum	*You Try It* 2.5 Understanding Counterarguments
Video 2.6 Double-Column Notebook	Sample Paper Cole Essay Excerpt	*You Try It* 2.6 Analyzing Visual Images
Video 2.7 Critical Reading of a Text	Sample Paper Journal Page	

Video 2.8 Using the Checklist for Critical Reading	Sample Paper Double-Column Notebook	
Video 2.9 Terrorism Highway Sign	Sample Paper Sacks Essay	
Video 2.10 Saturn SUV Advertisement	Checklist Critical Reading	
Video 2.11 Checklist for Critical Viewing	Sample Image DC Beltway Terrorism Sign	
	Sample Image SUV Advertisement	
	Checklist Critical Viewing	

Chapter Highlights

This chapter begins with a general description of critical thinking, including these distinct processes: establishing your purpose and raising questions, analyzing the topic, synthesizing, making inferences, and evaluating. It then devotes most of its attention to active reading. Using an essay about sex discrimination in high school and college athletics for illustration, it shows students how to read on three different levels: reading for literal meaning, reading for interpretation, and reading critically (evaluative reading). The latter is divided into two subtypes—internal evaluation and external evaluation—and this is the heart of the chapter. For this chapter to work best, you should familiarize your students with the basics of Title IX. The chapter continues with suggestions on how to structure the reading process (previewing, reading, and reviewing) and on how to annotate and summarize a text. The chapter concludes with a section on critical viewing, which encourages students to use the same three-level type of analysis they should use for reading: viewing for literal meaning, viewing for interpretation, and viewing critically.

Learning Outcomes

The learning outcomes for Chapter 2 are listed in the following chart, along with the relevant sections of the chapter and exercises that teachers can use to evaluate their students' mastery of the objectives. This chart also appears as a clickable link in the etext.

CHAPTER 2 LEARNING OUTCOMES CHART	
To assess your understanding of the Chapter 2 learning outcomes, work the corresponding You Try It exercises and study the relevant chapter sections.	
2.1 Use reading and writing for inquiry, learning, thinking, and communicating.	*You Try It*: 2.1 Critical Analysis of a Purchase *You Try It*: 2.2 Analyzing Audience and Purpose
2.2 Read actively and critically, using evaluative standards to help understand what you read.	*You Try It*: 2.3 Inferences *You Try It*: 2.5 Understanding Counterarguments
2.3 View images actively and critically, distinguishing between the literal and rhetorical meaning of images.	*You Try It*: 2.6 Analyzing Visual Images

2.1 **Think critically**

Teaching Suggestions

This section of the chapter describes the systematic approach to knowledge building that all instructors seek to instill in students—critical thinking. The concept is only briefly introduced here; however, critical thinking skills are discussed many times throughout the etext. I suggest that you help students see that the thinking habits they develop during their college years will be useful throughout their lives.

2.2 **Read actively and critically**

Teaching Suggestions

As you work with this section of the chapter, help students realize that when they read, they are actually making meaning on three different levels. Discuss with students the important links among reading, writing, and thinking. Try to help them become more aware of their own literacy practices and how those practices are interconnected. When students write about what they have read, they come to understand it better. When they read their own and others' writing, they learn about the reading and writing processes.

Encourage students to read slowly and carefully, reviewing difficult texts several times and annotating them in detail. These are skills that take practice and patience to develop. Similarly, encourage students to slow down their writing process, thinking critically at each stage in an effort to understand and control the process better. You might share your own writing experiences with students as you work together to gain a better understanding of this complex process. Learning to be a critical reader is even more important in this age of sound bites, twitter feeds, and slogans. Students know how to browse and skim from countless hours spent online. What they often don't know is how to read slowly and deeply.

Class Activities

Provide students with a brief article and have them practice annotating it. Give them about fifteen minutes to read and annotate. Then, have them gather into groups to compare their annotations. Were there major differences? Discuss the results of this activity with the entire class. Did students in each group arrive at the same key ideas for the piece? This activity can be shared online.

Computer Activities

Have students create a double-column notebook on their computer, as described in this section of the chapter.

2.3 **Engage actively and critically in the viewing process**

Connections

Look over Chapter 4, "Formulating Arguments," to see if there are places where you can draw connections for students. For example, you could have your students analyze the Joe Chemo ad, noting how the social context likely influences the reader's reaction.

Answers for Chapter 2 *You Try It* Exercises

For the exercises in this chapter, answers will vary.

Additional Exercise

Have students bring in to class a glossy magazine advertisement built around a striking image. Working in small groups, have them analyze the image and the advertisement using the "Checklist for Critical Viewing." This exercise can also be done online using a discussion forum or chat room to share information.

CHAPTER 3 / *The Writing Process*

MULTIMEDIA FOR CHAPTER 3

Video Tutorials	Sample Documents	Writing Activities
Video 3.1 Chapter Introduction	Guidelines Stages of the Writing Process	*You Try It* 3.1 Exploring Topics
Video 3.2 Stages of Writing	Sample Interpretive Essay Assignment	*You Try It* 3.2 Outlining a Rhetorical Stance
Video 3.3 Exploring Topics on the Internet	Sample Executive Summary Assignment	*You Try It* 3.3 Brainstorming
Video 3.4 Constructing Your Rhetorical Stance	Checklist Constructing Your Rhetorical Stance	*You Try It* 3.4 Freewriting
Video 3.5 Various Types of Media with Different Audiences	Sample Kirsten's Rhetorical Stance	*You Try It* 3.5 Invisible Writing
Video 3.6 Using a Computer Journal	Sample Image Facebook Post	*You Try It* 3.6 Clustering
Video 3.7 Avoiding Plagiarism	Sample Image Email	*You Try It* 3.7 Debating

Video 3.8 Organizing Your Files	Sample Image Blog Post	*You Try It* 3.8 Googling
Video 3.9 Taking Notes Using the Document Comment Feature	Sample Two Title Pages	*You Try It* 3.9 Discussing Topics
Video 3.10 Evaluating a Working Thesis	Sample Headings and Subheadings	*You Try It* 3.10 Browsing Periodicals
Video 3.11 Choosing a Research Topic	Checklist Evaluating a Working Thesis	*You Try It* 3.11 Narrowing Your Topic
Video 3.12 Writing a Thesis Statement	Sample Paper Organizing by Time- Process Description	*You Try It* 3.12 Formulating a Working Thesis
Video 3.13 Outlining with a Computer	Sample Paper Organizing by Space	*You Try It* 3.13 Evaluating and Revising Your Working Thesis
Video 3.14 Combining Documents with Windows	Sample Paper Organizing by Logic	*You Try It* 3.14 Organizing Your Information
Video 3.15 Storyboards	Sample PowerPoint Storyboard	*You Try It* 3.15 Outline Practice
Video 3.16 Overcoming Writer's Block	Guidelines Overcoming Writer's Block	*You Try It* 3.16 Drafting a Document

Video 3.17 Collaborating via Computer	Sample Paper Kirsten's Net Theft Draft	*You Try It* 3.17 Analyzing Your Writing Process
Video 3.18 Student Draft with Instructor Comments		*You Try It* 3.18 Writing Collaboratively

Chapter Highlights

This chapter guides students through the writing process, introducing both rhetorical principles and many invention and prewriting techniques. Several videos show ways in which computers can help writers during the writing process.

Learning Outcomes

The learning outcomes for Chapter 3 are listed in the following chart, along with the relevant sections of the chapter and exercises that teachers can use to evaluate their students' mastery of the objectives. This chart also appears as a clickable link in the etext.

CHAPTER 3 LEARNING OUTCOMES CHART	
To assess your understanding of the Chapter 3 learning outcomes, work the corresponding You Try It exercises and study the relevant chapter sections.	
3.1 Use multiple drafts to create and complete a successful project.	*You Try It*: 3.16 Drafting a Document
3.2 Employ flexible strategies for composing, revising, editing, and proofreading.	*You Try It*: 3.17 Analyzing Your Writing Process

3.3 Understand writing as an open, recursive process.	*You Try It:* 3.1 Exploring Topics *You Try It:* 3.11 Narrowing Your Topic
3.4 Understand the collaborative and social nature of the writing process.	*You Try It:* 3.9 Discussing Topics Study Chapter 3.7a
3.5 Critique yourself and others.	Study Chapter 3.8
3.6 Be responsible for your part of a team effort.	*You Try It:* 3.18 Writing Collaboratively
3.7 Use a variety of technologies for various audiences and purposes.	Study the chapter's Tech Help videos

3.1 Overview of the writing process

Teaching Suggestions

It is always tempting when teaching a writing class to tell students the "right way" to do things based on your own experience. However, there are many types of learners and many ways to learn—for example, some learners are visual, while others are aural. Students should approach every writing assignment with a spirit of experimentation, ready to explore, invent, and discover along the way. Instructors should not close off creativity and original thinking by forcing students into one mode of learning. Students need to understand, however, that tools exist that all writers can employ to write better.

3.2 Experiment and explore

Teaching Suggestions

As the chapter mentions, experienced writers tend to spend a great deal more time on exploration than do novices. Students should be encouraged not to come to closure on their explorations too early. This section of the chapter encourages students to consider their rhetorical stance (topic, audience, purpose, persona) and genre, language, and design options, all in the spirit of experimentation.

Class Activities

1. Bring to class copies of a short newspaper or news magazine article on a timely topic. Read the article together as a class. Then analyze the article's rhetorical stance: What is the topic? What logical arguments are used? Who is the persona? Who is the audience? How might the piece be different if any one of these were changed? Have students describe a different rhetorical stance that would result in a very different piece. These descriptions can be shared in small groups or with the entire class. This activity may be done in an online discussion forum.

2. Have students draft a short paragraph, on a topic of their choice, geared to a general audience. Then have students redraft their paragraphs for a more specific audience (for example, peers, parents, friends, church groups, civic groups, or political groups). You may even have students experiment with how differently they would write this paragraph's information when texting a friend. This activity may also be done in a computer classroom or online discussion forum.

3. Bring to class or post at your class website a short excerpt from an article or essay in which the author's tone (perhaps ironic or sarcastic) is clearly apparent. Have students discuss (in person or online) what they consider the tone to be. Try to identify, as a group, some language choices in the piece that contribute to that tone. For comparison purposes, you might want to look at another excerpt that exhibits a very different tone. If you are in a traditional classroom, the excerpts can be projected on an overhead for comparison.

Collaborative Activities

1. Ask students to write a one-paragraph audience profile for an essay they plan to write. Have them describe as completely as they can the audience they envision. After they have written a first draft of the essay itself, have the students exchange drafts (in person or online) and write an audience profile for another student's essay.

2. Have students gather in small groups to discuss possible topic options. Use the two sample assignments in this section as a springboard for discussion. You might want to copy one of them onto a transparency

and project it for the class to refer to during discussion. This activity may also be done in an online discussion forum.

Computer Activities

1. Project on an LCD an example of a file management program such as Windows Explorer. Demonstrate for students how files can be organized into folders and directories on their own disks. Suggest an organizational scheme that will accommodate the major assignments for your course, and have students create appropriate folders.

2. Conduct a model Internet search to find an interesting topic to write about. Have students turn off their monitors and observe your demonstration on the LCD. Once they have seen you conduct a search, encourage them to explore topic options individually on the Internet.

3.3 Invent and prewrite

Teaching Suggestions

This section of the chapter provides students with numerous suggestions on preparing for writing. Working through these various options can help students understand the many diverse approaches to preparation that are possible—and perhaps add a few of their own that I have not thought of! Many invention activities can be done either independently or as a group. Encourage students to collaborate as they prewrite. Remind them that, whenever they are beginning any writing project, they can return to these prewriting techniques to generate ideas about their topics.

Class Activities

1. Introduce students to brainstorming by using class time to practice the technique. Choose a topic that is currently of concern on your campus (for example, parking or food service). Then note ideas on the board as students call them out to you. Keep the brainstorming open and free-flowing as long as the students have ideas to share. Then ask them to begin categorizing the ideas on the board in an effort to convert important ideas into headings and related ideas into subheadings. Discuss how brainstorming can be used as a way to inventory students' existing knowledge about a topic and to generate ideas.

38

2. Using the same approach as in Activity 1, introduce clustering by using class time to practice the technique.

3. Encourage students to keep a writing journal in which they freewrite for ten minutes each day. Occasionally, take class time for freewriting, especially when students are first beginning a writing project.

4. As a class, have students write preliminary thesis statements for a topic of your choice. Working as a group often helps students better understand the concept behind writing a thesis.

5. All of the above activities may be adapted for an online class using classroom tools such as discussion forums, file-sharing spaces, and chat rooms.

Collaborative Activities

Conduct a debate activity, as described in 3.3e. Have students take sides on a topic, and then choose three to four spokespersons for each position. Line up two sets of chairs in the front of the room, and let the students debate one another. Designate audience members as scorekeepers, if desired. Encourage students to restrict the debate to the topic. Use this activity to help students understand the need to consider arguments counter to their own as they write. This activity may also be conducted in an online discussion forum or chat room.

Computer Activities

1. Introduce students to the DOCUMENT COMMENTS function of whatever word processing program they are using. Encourage students to share prewriting files (brainstorming or freewriting) and to comment on each other's early, exploratory work. Comments can be inserted into the document itself using the word processing program's commenting feature. Be sure to have students save the comments file under a different name (for example, "Brandon's comments for José.doc").

2. Encourage students to try brainstorming, freewriting, and invisible writing at the computer.

3. Use a computer drawing program to carry out a clustering activity similar to the one illustrated in the chapter. Encourage students to experiment with a variety of visual designs. Compare the designs, and

discuss conclusions as a class. If possible, display the completed drawings on an LCD.

4. Help students set up a personal blog as an electronic journal at a free site such as WordPress.com. Be sure to explain that blogs are open to public viewing and discuss appropriate personal security protocol.

Connections

For an interesting discussion of the importance of prewriting, see Peter Elbow, *Writing Without Teachers* (New York: Oxford UP, 1973). See also W. Ross Winterowd, "Rhetorical Invention," *The Allyn and Bacon Sourcebook for College Writing Teachers*, ed. James C. McDonald (Boston: Allyn & Bacon, 1996).

3.4 Gather information but avoid plagiarism

Teaching Suggestions

Often, students and instructors immediately head to Google for an Internet search when a writing task needs outside sources. Certainly, the Internet is an extremely important place for information. But neither you nor your students should neglect other sources, particularly at the early, formative stages of the writing process. This section of the chapter suggests that students begin with informal discussions and brainstorming before moving on to more formal searching. Browsing through interesting journals, "Googling" topics, and skimming library databases can help students get started on an outside search. Finding and using sources appropriately is covered at length in Part 4 of the etext.

Class Activities

1. Discuss with students the difference between writing a paper based on their own knowledge and writing a paper using sources. Make them aware of the many resources for research writing provided in Part 4 of the etext.

2. Encourage students to interview an expert on their chosen topic. Have students report their interview results to the class. Interviews may be conducted via email or online chat.

Computer Activities

Model an Internet search for your class, showing them how to use a variety of search tools and key words to achieve differing results. Refer students to Chapter 17 for more detailed information on searching the Internet.

3.5 **Plan and organize**

Teaching Suggestions

Although students are probably aware of the concept of writing a thesis and an outline, many of them are not in the habit of doing so. As is often the case with writing processes, students need practice to master these techniques. In this section of the chapter, students are encouraged to practice thesis writing by revising and rewriting a working thesis. As they review and discuss various iterations of the thesis, they will become better at understanding its purpose and power for writers. Similarly, when they practice outlining, students will become better able to see the benefits of organizing and shaping their thoughts. Ask students to peer-review each other's thesis statements and outlines early in the process so that they receive additional feedback.

Class Activities

1. Devote considerable time in class to having students write, rewrite, and evaluate thesis statements. Put "Evaluating a Working Thesis" on a transparency to show on an overhead projector. Ask students to think critically about the three sample thesis statements. Then, give the students dry-erase markers and have them write their own thesis statements on blank transparencies for the class to discuss. Encourage students to help one another narrow and focus their thesis statements. This activity may be done in an online discussion forum.

2. Bring to class or post to your online classroom various sample paragraphs that illustrate organization by time, space, and logic. If you are in a classroom, show these models on an overhead projector and discuss the organizational strategies used. Ask students to bring in for discussion or post to the class website other models that illustrate these patterns. Refer students to Chapter 5 for a lengthy consideration of logical patterns.

3. Bring to class or post to your online classroom sample essays by professional writers, and ask students to outline them. They may discover that some essays do not have a clear structure, which may lead to some interesting discussions about the various ways in which writing can be effective. And when they compare their outlines (either in person or online), they may discover that different students identified different emphases and orders for development.

4. Bring to class or post to your online classroom an outline that has been scrambled—that is, the headings and subheadings have been rearranged. Ask students to reorder the headings and subheadings so that they make sense. Discuss and compare the students' outlines. This activity can also be done in an online discussion forum.

3.6 Compose a draft

Teaching Suggestions

Many writers fall into habits that do not involve the reflection necessary for successful writing. Try to help students understand their own habits and perhaps try out some new methods of composing that they had not thought of before. This section of the chapter suggests two such methods: the building block and top-down approaches to composing. Although these certainly are not the only possibilities, they do open the composing process to scrutiny and self-reflection.

Class Activities

1. Spend a few minutes having students reflect on their own composing processes. Have them write in their journals a brief paragraph describing a typical process they used when drafting a recent writing assignment in another class. As a group, talk about their experiences and suggest some other ways of composing that might be more productive. This activity may be done in an online discussion forum.

2. Discuss experiences of writer's block that students have had in the past. What methods did they use to overcome the block? Look together at the "Ways to Overcome Writer's Block." Have any of these guidelines worked for students in the past? Can they offer additional suggestions? This activity may be done in an online discussion forum.

Computer Activities

In a computer classroom, have students compose in building blocks from their outline. Or, alternatively, have them compose top down, using their thesis statements as a guide. Encourage them to use any text-building features available in the word processing software as they compose.

3.7 **Collaborate**

Teaching Suggestions

Many writing instructors make productive use of collaboration at all stages of the writing process, either in class or online. Composing does not have to be a solitary enterprise. Rather, students can be encouraged to compose together in writing groups or teams. As the instructor, you should help students with group dynamics and with group roles. With clearly assigned tasks and roles as described in this section of the chapter, students can work together harmoniously and produce effective writing. I suggest that you give group members some of the responsibility for evaluating each other's work. I have found in my own teaching that students are extremely perceptive and fair when judging one another's contributions to a group project.

Collaborative Activities

Assign students to groups for a collaborative writing project. Provide them with suggested roles—for example, group leader, group librarian, group publisher, and group reporter—but allow them the freedom to decide who will be responsible for which roles.

Computer Activities

Use the collaborative exercise outlined in *You Try It* 3.18 to give students practice in composing together. When students have completed the exercise, have them discuss their feelings about composing together. Can they imagine any real-world scenarios where several people might need to compose together at a computer?

Connections

For an excellent overview of collaborative learning, see Harvey S. Weiner, "Collaborative Learning in the Classroom: A Guide to Evaluation," *College English* 48 (Jan. 1986): 52–61. See also Lisa Ede and Andrea Lunsford, "The

43

Pedagogy of Collaboration," *The Allyn & Bacon Sourcebook for College Writing Teachers*, ed. James C. McDonald (Boston: Allyn & Bacon, 1996).

3.8 **Review a student draft**

Teaching Suggestions

Reading through the model student essay together in class is a good way to begin a discussion about the draft's strengths and weaknesses. First, make sure that the students understand the essay's arguments. Make a listing on the blackboard or in a discussion forum of students' thoughts about the strengths and the weaknesses of the essay. Discuss the instructor's comments on the draft as well. What are the comments asking the writer to do? Do the instructor's suggestions seem reasonable? This essay reappears in Chapter 6 in its revised version; you may want to alert students that they will be returning to this essay to see how it was rewritten by its author.

Computer Novice Notes

Novices will need extra practice with blocking text and using the CUT, COPY, PASTE and CLICK AND DRAG functions of their word processing program. They will also need to learn how to use the SAVE AS function. Once again, it is important that those new to using computers understand that they can save the same file in different locations on various disk drives or Web locations; in various formats, such as HTML (hypertext markup language) or RTF (rich text format); and in the same location but with different names. They will need to become familiar with the various file-saving options available in the word processing program your class is using. It is important to practice using these functions early in the term so that students are comfortable with essential aspects of word processing.

Computer Activities

Introduce students to the outline feature that is available on the word processing software they are using. Have students practice generating an outline, using the outlining feature.

ESL Note

Many nonnative speakers of English come from cultures in which linear arguments are not the norm. They may not have had much experience with the typical organizational patterns used by Western writers—a thesis statement followed by a linear progression of main points supported by sub-points. Teachers of nonnative speakers need to pay particular attention to helping students understand the construction of essays in English; such essays require a title, an introduction and a thesis, the development of key ideas in a linear progression, appropriate transitions between main ideas, and a conclusion.

Computer Novice Notes

Novice computer users may have a difficult time at first understanding how the files, folders, and directories are organized in their computer drives. You may need to spend time helping these users learn to save their work to a disk drive, name their files, and retrieve them later from a classroom drive. Although this process appears self-evident to those who have used computers for a long time, to a beginner it can be baffling. Similarly, when teaching online, you will need to spend considerable time orienting your class to the online classroom tools you will be using in your class. It is helpful to begin a nuts-and-bolts discussion forum at the start of class to provide a location where students can ask those technical questions that will inevitably arise. Don't be afraid to pick up the phone and call a student if you feel he or she is struggling. Sometimes talking them through the situation on the phone is the best option.

Answers for Chapter 3 *You Try It* Exercises

For the exercises in this chapter, answers will vary.

Additional Exercises

Ask students to write a short paragraph organized by time and another organized by space. Then talk about these patterns of organization and how writers might use them. This activity may also be done in an online discussion forum.

Chapter 4 / *Formulating Arguments*

MULTIMEDIA FOR CHAPTER 4

VIDEO TUTORIALS	SAMPLE DOCUMENTS	WRITING ACTIVITIES
Video 4.1 Chapter Introduction	Sample Facebook Page	*You Try It* 4.1 Analyzing a Thesis
Video 4.2 Good Thesis Statement Examples	Checklist Formulating an Arguable Thesis	*You Try It* 4.2 Considering Purpose and Audience
Video 4.3 Formulating an Arguable Thesis	Sample Paper Interpretive Essay	*You Try It* 4.3 Using Evidence
Video 4.4 Inductive and Deductive Reasoning	Sample Paper Response Essay	*You Try It* 4.4 Opposing Points of View
Video 4.5 Working Through a Thesis	Example Factual Data	*You Try It* 4.5 Analyzing a Point
Video 4.6 Two Genre Examples	Example Expert Opinion	*You Try It* 4.6 Build a Compelling Case
Video 4.7 Using Genre to Plan	Example Personal Experience	*You Try It* 4.7 Locating Fallacies
Video 4.8 Angela Napper's Arguments	Sample Paper Angela's Argument	*You Try It* 4.8 Practice the Five-Part Method

Video 4.9 Supporting Evidence	Example Illustrative Examples	*You Try It* 4.9 Practice the Problem and Solution Method
Video 4.10 Pro/Con Paper	Checklist Supporting Evidence	*You Try It* 4.10 Practice the Rogerian Method
Video 4.11 An Analysis of Angela's Claim	Sample Paper Angela's Counterevidence	*You Try It* 4.11 Practice the Narrative Method
Video 4.12 Sound Reasoning	Sample Paper Pro/Con Debate	*You Try It* 4.12 Outline Angela's Paper
Video 4.13 Logical Patterns	Checklist Sound Reasoning	*You Try It* 4.13 Practice Electronic Argument
Video 4.14 Establishing Your Ethos	Sample Kirsten's Revision Outline	*You Try It* 4.14 Finding Visual Support
Video 4.15 Speech with Obvious Fallacy	Table: Toulmin Analysis of Angela's Claim	
Video 4.16 Overgeneralization and Oversimplification	Guidelines Common Logical Patterns	
Video 4.17 Begging the Question	Sample Paper Angela's Argument	
Video 4.18 Attacking the Person	Sample Paper Problem/Solution Memo	

Video 4.19 Either/Or Reasoning	Sample Paper Kirsten's Rogerian Argument	
Video 4.20 Faulty Cause and Effect Reasoning	Sample Paper Kirsten's Narrative Argument	
Video 4.21 Using False Analogies	Guidelines Designing a Web Argument	
Video 4.22 Bandwagon Appeals	Sample A Website Argument	
Video 4.23 Red Herrings	Sample A Visual Image	
Video 4.24 Two Wrongs Make a Right		
Video 4.25 Appealing to Bias		
Video 4.26 Keeping Track of an Argument		
Video 4.27 Student Model with Obvious Structure		

Video 4.28 Designing a Web Argument		
Video 4.29 An Electronic Argument		
Video 4.30 A Visual Argument		
Video 4.31 Using Visuals in Support of an Argument		

Chapter Highlights

This chapter helps students construct good arguments. Using a student essay on cybercensorship as an example, it teaches students how to compose an arguable thesis, how to consider purpose and audience, how to generate good supporting evidence and consider counterevidence, how to develop and test main points, and how to build a compelling case. It also includes sections on different kinds of emotional and logical fallacies, on different ways to structure an argument, and on different forms of electronic argument. Finally, there is a section on visual argument, showing how visual images and language working together can produce a memorable and sometimes very effective argument.

Learning Outcomes

The learning outcomes for Chapter 4 are listed in the following chart, along with the relevant sections of the chapter and exercises that teachers can use to evaluate their students' mastery of the objectives. This chart also appears as a clickable link in the etext.

CHAPTER 4 LEARNING OUTCOMES CHART	
To assess your understanding of the Chapter 4 learning outcomes, work the corresponding You Try It exercises and study the relevant chapter sections.	
4.1 Respond appropriately to different rhetorical situations.	*You Try It*: 4.2 Considering Purpose and Audience
4.2 Understand how genre shapes writing.	Study Chapter 4.3
4.3 Build an argument while considering other points of view.	*You Try It*: 4.3 Using Evidence *You Try It*: 4.4 Opposing Points of View *You Try It*: 4.6 Build a Compelling Case
4.4 Structure an argument.	Study Chapter 4.9-4.11 and work *You Try It* exercises 4.8-4.14

Teaching Suggestions

Many students, especially those new to college, are not inclined to take a position and argue for it. Instead, they merely try to cover a topic. In some cases, of course, an instructor may ask only for coverage. But college writing—whether it concerns a literary work, a social issue, or an economic policy—often requires the more focused treatment that is characteristic of argumentation. As early as possible in their college careers, students need to develop the ability to formulate an argument. Look for opportunities to connect the material in this chapter with assignments they have in other courses. Ask students, for example, about essay exams or papers they have to write. Discuss with them the written arguments you have had to write, either inside or outside of academia.

Argumentation can be done gently and considerately, as a way of exploring an issue rather than beating someone. This is especially important in academia, where learning is the main goal; it would be a good topic for discussion.

You may also want to bring up cultural and gender differences. Sociologists and anthropologists have found that in some cultures, argumentation and public debate are seen as important ways of promoting social interaction; in others, they are seen as divisive and therefore best avoided. Likewise, some researchers have claimed that men are more comfortable engaging in public argument than are women, at least in the United States. See, for example, Deborah Tannen, *You Just Don't Understand* (New York: William Morrow, 1990).

4.1 Formulate an argument

Class Activities

Have each student devise a claim of his or her own, using the guidelines in An Arguable Thesis or Claim. Then have students gather in groups of two or three (in class or online) to analyze their claims according to the instructions for *You Try It* 4.1. Later, you may want to call on a couple of students to present their claims and analyses for full class discussion. This activity may be done in an online chat room or discussion forum.

4.2 Consider your purpose and audience

Connections

Considering one's purpose and audience is discussed at length in the section, "Considering your rhetorical stance." There it is talked about in general terms; here you have a good opportunity to show how that general advice can be applied to a specific situation, especially the cybercensorship argument being constructed by Angela Napper in section 4.3.

4.3 Consider the genre

Teaching Suggestion

Explore the sample papers included in this section of the chapter in order to help students understand how genre often shapes the content and development of an argument.

4.4 Generate good supporting evidence

Teaching Suggestions

Some kinds of evidence are more appropriate and effective than others in certain fields or certain kinds of writing. In engineering, for example, factual data are generally considered to be more important than personal experience. Ask your students to reflect on the other courses they are taking and then discuss the nature of evidence in those fields of study. This activity may be done in an online discussion forum or chat room.

4.5 Take note of evidence from alternative views

Connections

Presenting alternative views requires the careful use of conditional sentences in the subjunctive mood.

4.6 Develop and test your main points

Teaching Suggestions

A good way to show students the value of testing their main points is to have them present their ideas to some of their fellow students. Have students bring in an ordered list of points for a claim they want to make. Then divide the class up into groups of three students, and have each student present his or her points to the other two students in the group and get their reactions. It usually turns out to be a very instructive experience! This activity may be done in an online discussion forum or chat room.

4.7 Build a compelling case

Teaching Suggestions

The three different kinds of appeals (to logic, authority, and emotion) are often combined. Remind students that, as they analyze different texts, they should be sure not to overlook such combinations.

4.8 Avoid logical and emotional fallacies

Class Activities

Fallacies can be found in many types of public discourse—for example, in advertisements, in letters to the editor, and on radio talk shows. Have students collect some examples and bring them to class for discussion or post them on the class discussion forum.

Have students practice fallacies by writing them. You can make this activity into a game where students try to identify the obvious fallacies written by their classmates. This activity can be done in class or online via a discussion forum or chat room.

4.9 Structure the argument

Teaching Suggestions

This section's discussion of inductive versus deductive arrangement is not meant to be inflexible. There are situations—in a letter to the editor, for example—where a writer might want to use the deductive pattern, even though he or she is likely to encounter immediate resistance from readers. This would be a good topic for class discussion.

4.10 Electronic argument

Have students find an example of electronic argument on some listserv, newsgroup, or email conversation. Have them print it out and evaluate it according to the guidelines for designing a Web argument. These may be shared at your class's online classroom site.

4.11 **Visual argument**

Additional Exercise

Have students each find a public service advertisement like the Joe Chemo ad in this section or some other advertisement that presents an argument both visually and verbally. Have them analyze it using the guidelines laid out in this chapter. You may also want to have them use the Checklist for Critical Viewing.

Answers for Chapter 4 *You Try It* Exercises

➲ *YOU TRY IT* 4.1

Each claim requires a lengthy response, and many options are possible. I offer the following only as an example of an appropriate response to the claim "U2 is the best musical group ever."

Debatable? Yes. Many music fans would disagree.

Supportable with readily available evidence? Yes, if "best" is defined by record sales or a similar metric.

Open to counterarguments? Probably. Opponents could argue for the superiority of some other group, using some metric or definition that doesn't favor U2.

Clearly stated claim? As worded, it is a clearly stated claim of value, although the term "musical group" could mean different things to different people.

Personal opinion only? Not really. Although it could be the arguer's personal opinion, it could well be shared by many other people.

The proponent of this claim could marshal evidence from record sales, number of hit songs, number of weeks on the pop charts, or some other metric—whatever might favor U2. An opponent could look to similar sorts of measures if they *don't* favor U2.

➲ *You Try Its* 4.2–4.9 Answers will vary.

Chapter 5 / *Structuring Paragraphs*

MULTIMEDIA FOR CHAPTER 5

VIDEO TUTORIALS	SAMPLE DOCUMENTS	WRITING ACTIVITIES
Video 5.1 Chapter Introduction	Chart Patterns of Organization	*You Try It* 5.1 Finding the Topic Sentences
Video 5.2 Unifying Paragraphs with Topic Sentences	Guidelines Transitional Words and Phrases	*You Try It* 5.2 Placing the Topic Sentence
Video 5.3 Placing the Topic Sentence	Example Effective Introductions	*You Try It* 5.3 General to Specific
Video 5.4 General to Specific	Example Effective Conclusions	*You Try It* 5.4 Cause and Effect
Video 5.5 Cause and Effect	Guidelines Effective Introductions and Conclusions	*You Try It* 5.5 Compare and Contrast
Video 5.6 Compare and Contrast		*You Try It* 5.6 Definition
Video 5.7 Definition		*You Try It* 5.7 Classification
Video 5.8 Classification		*You Try It* 5.8 Problem and Solution

Video 5.9 Problem and Solution		*You Try It* 5.9 Narration or Process Description
Video 5.10 Narration or Process Description		*You Try It* 5.10 Exemplification
Video 5.11 Exemplification		*You Try It* 5.11 Physical or Spatial Description
Video 5.12 Physical or Spatial Description		*You Try It* 5.12 Mixing Patterns
Video 5.13 Mixing Patterns		*You Try It* 5.13 Using Transitions
Video 5.14 Transitional Words and Phrases		*You Try It* 5.14 Repeating Key Words
Video 5.15 Consistent Verb Tenses		*You Try It* 5.15 Using Old and New Information
Video 5.16 Parallelism		*You Try It* 5.16 Paragraph Techniques
Video 5.17 Appropriate Paragraph Length		*You Try It* 5.17 Connecting Links
Video 5.18 Linking Paragraphs		*You Try It* 5.18 Introductory and Concluding Paragraphs

Video 5.19 Introductory Paragraphs		
Video 5.20 Concluding Paragraphs		
Video 5.21 Introductions and Conclusions		

Chapter Highlights

Paragraphs are the primary building blocks of extended prose, each serving to develop a particular idea. This chapter covers the basic principles of good paragraph construction. It tells students how to write unified, coherent, and fully developed paragraphs and how to link paragraphs together. Its main emphasis is on different ways of organizing information in a paragraph and on the linguistic devices that are most suitable to specific patterns of organization.

Learning Outcomes

The learning outcomes for Chapter 5 are listed in the following chart, along with the relevant sections of the chapter and exercises that teachers can use to evaluate their students' mastery of the objectives. This chart also appears as a clickable link in the etext.

CHAPTER 5 LEARNING OUTCOMES CHART

To assess your understanding of the Chapter 5 learning outcomes, work the corresponding You Try It exercises and study the relevant chapter sections.

5.1 Use conventions of paragraph structure that are appropriate to the rhetorical situation.	*You Try It:* 5.1 Finding the Topic Sentences *You Try It:* 5.2 Placing the Topic Sentence
5.2 Employ common formats for structuring paragraphs.	*You Try It:* 5.3-5.12
5.3 Use appropriate sentence structures to produce unified, coherent paragraphs.	*You Try It:* 5.13-5.17
5.4 Write effective introductions and conclusions.	*You Try It:* 5.18 Introductory and Concluding Paragraphs

5.1 **Write unified paragraphs**

Teaching Suggestion

Find a published text (perhaps from a textbook) containing three or four well-written paragraphs on an interesting topic. Blank out the topic sentences, and then have students try to reconstruct them. Discuss their attempts and the reasons behind them. Then show the original sentences. This activity may be done in an online discussion forum.

5.2 **Write coherent paragraphs with clear patterns of organization**

Teaching Suggestion

Use this section of the chapter to have your students practice writing a variety of sentence patterns. Each pattern is described in the etext, followed by video examples and *You Try It* exercises. The chapter is organized to promote the "explore, engage, apply" teaching strategy. You can have students share their responses in class or online in a discussion forum.

Have students exchange their paragraphs (either in class or online) and try to identify the patterns used by their classmates. The more practice you can give students with patterns the more comfortable they will be with using them in their own paragraphs.

ESL Note

Patterns of paragraph organization can differ from one culture to another. For example, scholastic paragraphs in some Asian cultures tend to circle around a topic rather than address it directly, while those in Arabic cultures tend to use elaborate parallelism and paraphrasing (R. Kaplan, "Cultural Thought Patterns Revisited," *Writing Across Languages: Analyzing L2 Texts*, ed. U. Connor and R. Kaplan [Boston: Addison-Wesley, 1986]).

5.3 Write coherent paragraphs with sentence-linking techniques

Teaching Suggestion

Allow students to practice using transitional words and phrases to link sentences within their own paragraphs. Working through the *You Try It* exercises in this section of the chapter will help students to identify and use transitions in their own writing.

Linguistic Note

In research literature, *old information* is sometimes referred to as *given information*. The principle of constructing sentences so that old information precedes new information is sometimes called *the given-new contract*.

5.4 Be consistent with verb tense, person, and number

Teaching Suggestion

Have students analyze some well-written published paragraphs for consistency of verb tense, person, and number. Then have them analyze some paragraphs in their own writing and compare the results. If you are teaching online, post the paragraphs in your classroom's file sharing space or online discussion forum.

5.5 Use parallelism to make paragraphs coherent

Teaching Suggestions

If students are unfamiliar with the term parallelism, it would be beneficial to give a quick introduction to the concept, using Chapter 11.

5.6 Decide on appropriate paragraph length

Class Activities

Find an interesting and reasonably well-written text that is several paragraphs in length, and reformat it into a single block of prose. (Downloading text from the Internet will make the reformatting easy.) Show the reformatted text to students, tell them how many paragraph breaks it originally had, and have them try to identify where those breaks were. If you are teaching online, post the paragraph in your classroom's file sharing space or discussion forum.

5.7 Link paragraphs with key words

Teaching Activity

Have students examine the two paragraphs in section 5.6 and determine what linguistic devices the etext author has used to link the second paragraph to the first. (Answer: Use of the transitional word *also* and use of old information in the term *desirable paragraph length.*)

5.8 Construct effective introductory and concluding paragraphs

Additional Exercise

Have students find an essay of their own, preferably one recently written, and analyze it for its opening and concluding paragraphs using the guidelines given in this section. If these paragraphs are inadequate, have them rewrite them. Students may share their opening and concluding paragraphs with each other via a discussion forum or file sharing space.

Answers for Chapter 5 *You Try It* Exercises

⊃ *You Try Its* 5.1–5.2 Answers will vary.

⊃ *You Try It* 5.3

The original paragraph was as follows:

1. Of course I was religious
2. I grew up in the church.
3. So I didn't have much choice.
4. My father is a preacher, my grandfather was a preacher, my great-grandfather was a preacher, my only bother is a preacher, my daddy's brother is a preacher.

⊃ *You Try It* 5.4-5.11 Answers will vary.

⊃ *You Try It* 5.12

Topic Sentence 1: definition
Topic Sentence 2: cause and effect
Topic Sentence 3: cause and effect
Topic Sentence 4: definition, classification
Topic Sentence 5: definition, exemplification

⊃ *You Try Its* 5.13-18 Answers will vary.

Chapter 6 / Rewriting

MULTIMEDIA FOR CHAPTER 6

VIDEO TUTORIALS	SAMPLE DOCUMENTS	WRITING ACTIVITIES
Video 6.1 Chapter Introduction	Checklist Critical Reading Questions for Revision	*You Try It* 6.1 Preparing a Revision Outline
Video 6.2 Critical Reading Questions for Revision	Chart Major Elements of Writing	*You Try It* 6.2 Revising for Focus
Video 6.3 Revising your Document	Sample Brochure	*You Try It* 6.3 Revising for Coherence
Video 6.4 Preparing a Revision Outline	Sample Newsletter	*You Try It* 6.4 Revising for Organization
Video 6.5 Rewriting Your Document Using "Track Changes"	Checklist Editing	*You Try It* 6.5 Revising Openings and Closings
Video 6.6 Revising for Focus	Checklist Grammar Checker Rules	*You Try It* 6.6 Editing Practice
Video 6.7 Using a Grammar Checker Appropriately	Checklist Proofreading Strategies	*You Try It* 6.7 Proofreading Practice

Video 6.8￼ Checking Sentence Structure	Checklist￼ Peer Response	*You Try It* 6.8￼ Giving Peer Feedback
Video 6.9￼ Checklist for Editing	Sample Paper￼ Kirsten's Revised Essay	*You Try It* 6.9￼ Receiving Peer Feedback
Video 6.10￼ Editing for Sentence Structure		
Video 6.11￼ Editing for Wordiness		
Video 6.12￼ Editing Your Verbs		
Video 6.13￼ Grammar Checker Rules		
Video 6.14￼ Proofreading Strategies		
Video 6.15￼ Proofreading on Screen and in Print		
Video 6.16￼ Peer Review: An Introduction		
Video 6.17￼ Email Comments to a Peer		

Video 6.18 Using CAPS to Comment		
Video 6.19 Using Document Comments for Peer Review		
Video 6.20 Using Footnotes for Peer Review		
Video 6.21 Peer Response Checklist		
Video 6.22: Peer Review: Global Responses		
Video 6.23 Peer Review: Local Responses		
Video 6.24 Revising After Peer Review		
Video 6.25 Kirsten's Revised Net Theft Essay		

Chapter Highlights

Even though the etext separates the writing process into major stages and discusses them in separate chapters (Chapter 3 and Chapter 6), you should reinforce once again with students that this is a recursive process rather than a neat, linear one. This chapter on rewriting suggests strategies students can use to become effective revisers of their own writing. Often, students see revising simplistically, as "cleaning up" a draft. Or they see your request for rewriting as an indication of failure. Students should see rewriting as an essential and integral part of any writing project. This chapter encourages students to begin the rewriting stage by looking globally at their work, in order to revise for development, coherence, focus, organization, tone, and format. They should then edit their work for correctness. Finally, they should proofread for any distracting errors that might remain.

Learning Outcomes

The learning outcomes for Chapter 6 are listed in the following chart, along with the relevant sections of the chapter and exercises that teachers can use to evaluate their students' mastery of the objectives. This chart also appears as a clickable link in the etext.

CHAPTER 6 LEARNING OUTCOMES CHART	
To assess your understanding of the Chapter 6 learning outcomes, work the corresponding You Try It exercises and study the relevant chapter sections.	
6.1 Develop flexible strategies for revising, editing, and proofreading your own text.	*You Try It:* 6.2-6.5 *You Try It:* 6.6 Editing Practice *You Try It:* 6.7 Proofreading Practice
6.2 Shift from being a writer to being a reader of your own work.	*You Try It:* 6.1 Preparing a Revision Outline

| 6.3 Effectively critique each other's work by both giving and receiving feedback. | *You Try It:* 6.8 Giving Peer Feedback |
| | *You Try It:* 6.9 Receiving Peer Feedback |

Computer Novice Notes

Many of your students will already have discovered that word processing can make rewriting a draft much easier. Encourage the computer novices in your class to experiment with the CUT, COPY, PASTE, SEARCH, DOCUMENT COMMENTS, TRACK CHANGES and OUTLINE features as they rewrite their drafts. With practice, students' ability to use the power of word processing will improve.

6.1 Shift from writer to reader

Teaching Suggestions

It is often extremely difficult for students to read their own work objectively. They tend to read what they think they wrote, rather than what is actually on the page. Stress to students that they need to consciously shift the way they read their own writing in order to become objective critics of their own work.

Class Activities

Using model student essays projected on an overhead projector, show students how to critically read a draft. Discuss with them the elements of writing outlined in this section: focus, coherence, organization, development, tone, and format. It is important that students become familiar with these features and be able to determine when they are working well and when they are not. You should include model essays that show both good and poor examples of these features. Use the "Critical Reading Questions for Revision" checklist to structure your discussion.

Have students use the "Critical Reading Questions for Revision" checklist as a springboard for both self-review and peer review of a draft.

Using an overhead projector and a model student paper, work with students to construct a revision outline. Write with a dry-erase marker on the transparency as students decide together on an outline and make suggestions for how best to revise the model.

These activities may also be conducted in an online class, using the file sharing space and a discussion forum or chat room.

Computer Activities

Demonstrate for students the different word-processing tools they can use to change a text's appearance. Using an LCD projector, change the appearance of a text (spacing, fonts, page breaks, margins), and discuss how each change might help students gain the distance they need to more effectively revise their own work.

Project a model student paper on an LCD. Have the students, working as a class, outline the paper and then write a revision outline suggesting how the paper might be improved. Either type the outline right on the paper itself (using italics or all capital letters) or use two windows, one for the paper and the other for the outline.

6.2 Revise

Teaching Suggestions

Explain to students that revising is not some mysterious process, but rather a combination of three simple tasks: adding to a text, deleting from a text, and rearranging information within a text. Students become effective revisers when they learn how to perform each task to their best advantage. Knowing what to revise is the difficult part. However, if they have read their work critically and effectively, they should have several ideas about how to improve it through revisions. Encourage them to make substantial revisions in the structure, organization, and content of their work at this point in the rewriting process.

Class Activities

1. Practice the revision strategies outlined in this section with your class. You might project paragraphs overhead to revise as a class, having students look first for focus, then for coherence, organization, development, tone, and format. Encourage students to use the

"Revision Checklist" as they check their own work. This activity can also be done in a computer classroom or online using a file sharing space or discussion forum.

2. Project several openings and closings overhead for class discussion. Talk about the different types of openings and what makes them effective. Discuss when students might want to use summary conclusions and when speculative conclusions are preferable. Have students practice writing several titles, openings, and closings for the piece they are currently revising. Encourage experimentation and creativity in this activity. This activity can also be done in a computer classroom or online using a file-sharing space or discussion forum.

Collaborative Activities

Ask students to bring to class a newspaper or magazine article that they found to be enjoyable and well written. In small groups, have them share with each other the titles, opening paragraphs, and conclusions. They should discuss the author's choice of title and why the author began and ended in the ways he or she did. This activity can also be done in a computer classroom or online using a file-sharing space or discussion forum.

Computer Activities

1. Demonstrate for students the use of the DOCUMENT COMPARE feature of your word processing program. Encourage students to compare two drafts of their papers.

2. Turn on the TRACK CHANGES feature and track changes on a subsequent draft to demonstrate its use for your students.

Demonstrate for students how they might change the format of a paper to make it more visually appealing. Encourage experimentation with fonts, graphics, and colors so that students appreciate the range of possibilities. Discuss when such formats might be appropriate and when they might not. Stress that readability is ultimately the most important goal in formatting a text. Use the sample brochure and newsletter in 6.2f to begin the discussion.

Connections

For an interesting analysis of revising, see Nancy I. Sommers, "Revision Strategies of Student Writers and Experienced Adult Writers," CCC 31 (Dec. 1980): 378–88. See also Lester Faigley and Stephen Witte, "Analyzing Revision," *The Allyn & Bacon Sourcebook for College Writing Teachers*, ed. James C. McDonald (Boston: Allyn & Bacon, 1996).

6.3 **Edit**

Teaching Suggestions

Encourage students to turn to sentence-level editing only after rewriting has been largely completed. Sometimes students begin to edit too soon, before they have effectively rewritten their texts. Effective editing requires very careful, close reading as students check their sentence structure and verb usage and look for wordiness, repetition, and other errors, as summarized in the Editing Checklist.

Class Activities

1. Practice the editing strategies outlined in this section with your class. Project paragraphs overhead so that all the students can edit together, verifying correct sentence structure and verb usage and looking for wordiness, repetition, and other errors. This activity can also be done in a computer classroom or online using a file-sharing space or discussion forum.

2. Do appropriate sentence-level editing exercises, such as those in the sections listed in the "Editing Checklist."

3. Encourage students to use the "Editing Checklist" as they check their own work.

6.4 **Proofread**

Teaching Suggestions

Many of the errors in students' work are the result of ineffective or incomplete proofreading. Neatly typed pages from a word processor give the impression that a work is polished, when in fact it might still harbor errors. Students need to be encouraged to take responsibility for their own work. They should understand that, although word processing can help them prepare a final draft, they still need to proofread carefully for the many errors in mechanics and punctuation that spell-checkers and style/grammar-checkers will miss.

Class Activities

Discuss with your class (either in class or online) the proofreading strategies listed in this section. Which strategies have they tried? Which ones worked the best? Do they proofread on the screen, on a printed copy, or on both? Practice proofreading together, using model sentences or paragraphs projected overhead.

Computer Activities

Demonstrate for your class the proofreading strategies outlined in this section, using an LCD projector. Show students how to use different views of their work to gain distance and how to use the search function to check punctuation. If you have a text-reading program in your lab, demonstrate how the computer can slowly read the text aloud while you follow along and proofread.

6.5 Give and receive feedback electronically

Teaching Suggestions

Peer review groups are a hallmark of the modern writing class. Students need to learn that giving and receiving feedback are integral parts of the writing process. To make the peer review process effective, you must structure it for students. That is, you need to provide students with guidance in being both effective reviewers and receptive listeners. The more guidance you provide in effective peer review strategies, the better students will do. Especially important is providing students with questions or prompts to guide their reviews of one another's work. These prompts can be general, or they can relate specifically to features of the assignment that you will be evaluating. Be sure to discuss with students how the peer review process will work and what expectations you have for the experience. Will students read their work aloud to each other? Will they exchange written drafts? Will they comment via computer networks?

Class Activities

Discuss with your class appropriate peer review procedures, using the guidelines in "Giving Peer Feedback" and "Receiving Peer Feedback." You may wish to project these guidelines overhead. Be sure to discuss with your students the helpful student-to-student videos in this section of the chapter.

Collaborative Activities

Have students gather in groups of three or four for a read-around peer review session, in which each student reads his or her paper to the group members while they listen and take notes. Afterwards, group members give global feedback on the student's work. The global response prompts found in this section work well with this activity. You can arrange for read-around groups in your online class as well, using online chat.

Computer Activities

1. Ask students to email their drafts to you for your review and preliminary grading. Drafts should be emailed as file attachments that you can download and read on your office computer, or they should be posted at your class's file-sharing space. Use the DOCUMENT COMMENTS and TRACK CHANGES features to provide students with feedback, and then email the reviewed files back to the individual students.

2. Demonstrate for students how to save their work to a class website and how to exchange papers for review using those resources.

3. Demonstrate for students how to use their word processor's DOCUMENT COMMENTS and TRACK CHANGES features to peer review each other's work. Save the annotated document back to the class LAN.

Connections

For a seminal article on collaboration, see Kenneth Bruffee, "Collaborative Learning and 'The Conversation of Mankind,'" *College English* 56 (1984): 635–52.

6.5d Review a model student paper

Teaching Suggestions

Included in this section is a revised version of the same student paper shown in draft form in Chapter 4. Encourage students to compare the two versions and to discuss the ways in which the student rewrote the piece. How effective were the revisions? Did the student pay attention to the instructor's revision suggestions? Are there areas in which the paper could still be improved? Discussion may take place in person or online.

Answers for Chapter 6 *You Try It* Exercises

For all exercises in this chapter, answers will vary.

PART**TWO**

Rhetoric

CHAPTER 7 / *Reflecting*

MULTIMEDIA FOR CHAPTER 7

VIDEO TUTORIALS	SAMPLE DOCUMENTS	WRITING ACTIVITIES
Video 7.1 Chapter Introduction	3 Sample Reflective Documents	
Video 7.2 Reflection Model	Chart Five Reflective Genres	*You Try It* 7.1.1 Peer Conference Advice
Video 7.3 Family Story	Sample Paper Story	*You Try It* 7.1.2 Comparing the Guidelines to the Story
	Chart Key Features of a Story	*You Try It* 7.1.3 Practicing Outlining
	Flowchart Writing a Nonfiction Story	*You Try It* 7.1.4 Write a Story

Video 7.4 Memoir	Sample Paper Memoir	*You Try It* 7.2.1 Peer Conference Advice
	Chart Key Features of a Memoir	*You Try It* 7.2.2 Comparing the Guidelines to the Memoir
	Flowchart Writing a Memoir	*You Try It* 7.2.3 Practicing Outlining
		You Try It 7.2.4 Write a Memoir
Video 7.5 Profile Essay	Sample Paper Profile Essay	*You Try It* 7.3.1 Peer Conference Advice
	Chart Key Features of a Profile Essay	*You Try It* 7.3.2 Comparing the Guidelines to the Profile Essay
	Flowchart Writing a Profile Essay	*You Try It* 7.3.3 Practicing Outlining
		You Try It 7.3.4 Write a Profile Essay
Video 7.6 Montage Essay	Sample Paper Montage Essay	*You Try It* 7.4.1 Peer Conference Advice
	Chart Key Features of a Montage Essay	*You Try It* 7.4.2 Comparing the Guidelines to the Montage Essay

	Flowchart Writing a Montage Essay	*You Try It* 7.4.3 Practicing Outlining
		You Try It 7.4.4 Write a Montage Essay
Video 7.7 Blog	Sample Paper Blog Site	*You Try It* 7.5.1 Peer Conference Advice
	Chart Key Features of Blogs	*You Try It* 7.5.2 Comparing the Guidelines to the Blog
	Flowchart Writing a Blog	*You Try It* 7.5.3 Practicing Evaluating a Blog
		You Try It 7.5.4 Write a Blog

Chapter Highlights

Chapter 7 introduces students to various reflective genres of writing. Working through this chapter will help students to write their own reflective texts. The chapter encourages students to begin thinking about the aims or purposes for which they are writing and then moves to the genres that typically embody those types of texts. Teachers who generally use an "aims and modes" of writing approach in their writing classes will find this organization slightly different from what they might be used to. However, starting with purposes is similar to starting with aims for writing. I then move to genres of writing rather than to modes of writing because genres are the more typical way that writing is organized throughout the various disciplines in academia. For teachers who wish to discuss modes of writing, these are included as paragraph organizational patterns in Chapter 5.

The five genres of reflective writing covered in *Comp Online* are story, memoir, profile, montage, and blog. Of course, there are other reflective genres (e.g., poetry or plays). But I felt that the five genres represented here would give students a manageable introduction to reflective writing. Each of these models was taken from actual student papers written for actual college classes.

Learning Outcomes

The learning outcomes for Chapter 7 are listed in the following chart, along with the relevant sections of the chapter and exercises that teachers can use to evaluate their students' mastery of the objectives. This chart also appears as a clickable link in the etext.

CHAPTER 7 LEARNING OUTCOMES CHART	
To assess your understanding of the Chapter 7 learning outcomes, work the corresponding You Try It exercises and study the relevant chapter sections.	
7.1 Write various types of reflective texts.	*You Try It* 7.1.4 Write a Story *You Try It* 7.2.4 Write a Memoir *You Try It* 7.3.4 Write a Profile Essay *You Try It* 7.4.4 Write a Montage *You Try It* 7.5.4 Write a Blog
7.2 Communicate your thoughts and experiences to others.	*You Try It* 7.1.3-7.5.3

| 7.3 Explain the reasons for your values and beliefs. | Study Chapter 7.1-7.5 |
| 7.4 Focus your reflection around a key insight. | Study Chapter 7.1-7.5 |

Teaching Suggestions

As you think about setting up your course syllabus, look through this chapter to see which reflective genres you might want your students to write. These genres represent a range of difficulties, with the montage being perhaps the most challenging genre for students to write. Most likely, you are teaching a first-year composition course in which you will not have time to work through all of these genres with your students. However, you may be able to select one or two as an introduction to the reflective aim.

Many teachers find that assigning reflective writing early in the term helps students bridge the gap from writing they have done in high school to writing in college. The *You Try It* exercises for each genre help students to take a close look at the model student paper and to think through the key features of the genre. The last *You Try It* exercise in each section (7.1–7.5) of Chapter 7 culminates in writing a relatively brief reflective text using the genre features as a generative scaffold.

Class Activities

Many of the *You Try It* exercises and assignments will be completed by students individually. However, you can also use any of the exercises as class activities. Choose the ones that you think will help your students understand the concepts in the chapter. After you have selected a genre to assign, you might want to show the video and model student paper during class using an overhead projector. Walk through the model with your students, discussing the key features of the genre with them. If you have students outline the model or write a peer review of the model, use those assignments as a springboard for class discussions about the genre.

Collaborative Activities

Have students share their responses to the *You Try It* exercises in peer pairs or in small groups. If you are teaching in an online classroom, you can use a discussion forum or chat room for collaborative activities.

Connections

Parts 1 and 2 of *Comp Online* should be taught together. That is, once you have decided which genres in Chapter 7 you are going to assign, then fold in the chapters in Part 1 that will help students to actually write in that genre. When assigning a genre from Chapter 7, I would suggest also assigning students to work through Chapters 1 and 3 in Part 1.

Use Part 3 as you would a writing handbook. That is, when you see that your students are having problems with grammar and usage, take time to guide them through the relevant sections in Part 3 that will help them correct those problems in their writing. You can individualize your instruction to have students work toward solving problems specific to their own writing.

Answers for Chapter 7 *You Try It* Exercises and Assignments

For the exercises and assignments in this chapter, answers will vary.

CHAPTER 8 / *Evaluating*

MULTIMEDIA FOR CHAPTER 8

VIDEO TUTORIALS	SAMPLE DOCUMENTS	WRITING ACTIVITIES
Video 8.1￼Chapter Introduction	3 Sample Evaluative Documents Movie, Dance, Charities	
Video 8.2￼Web Evaluation	Chart Five Evaluative Genres	*You Try It* 8.1.1 Peer Conference Advice
Video 8.3￼Review Essay	Sample Paper Review Essay	*You Try It* 8.1.2 Comparing the Guidelines to the Review
	Chart Key Features of a Review	*You Try It* 8.1.3 Practicing Outlining
	Flowchart Writing a Review Essay	*You Try It* 8.1.4 Write a Review Essay
Video 8.4￼Response Essay	Sample Paper Response Essay	*You Try It* 8.2.1 Peer Conference Advice
	Chart Key Features of a Response Essay	*You Try It* 8.2.2 Comparing the Guidelines to the Response Essay

	Flowchart Writing a Response Essay	*You Try It* 8.2.3 Practicing Outlining
		You Try It 8.2.4 Write a Response Essay
Video 8.5 Interpretation Essay	Sample Paper Interpretive Essay	*You Try It* 8.3.1 Peer Conference Advice
	Chart Key Features of an Interpretive Essay	*You Try It* 8.3.2 Comparing the Guidelines to the Interpretive Essay
	Flowchart Writing an Interpretive Essay	*You Try It* 8.3.3 Using the Literary Present
		You Try It 8.3.4 Practicing Outlining
		You Try It 8.3.5 Write an Interpretive Essay
Video 8.6 Synthesis Essay	Sample Paper Synthesis Essay	*You Try It* 8.4.1 Peer Conference Advice
	Chart Key Features of Synthesis Essays	*You Try It* 8.4.2 Comparing the Guidelines to the Synthesis Essay
	Flowchart Writing a Synthesis Essay	*You Try It* 8.4.3 Practicing Outlining

		You Try It 8.4.4 Write a Synthesis Paper
Video 8.7 Short Report	Sample Paper Short Report	*You Try It* 8.5.1 Report Response
	Chart Key Features of Short Reports	*You Try It* 8.5.2 Comparing the Guidelines to the Report
	Flowchart Writing a Short Report	*You Try It* 8.5.3 Practicing Outlining a Report
		You Try It 8.5.4 Write a Short Report

Chapter Highlights

Chapter 8 introduces students to various evaluative genres of writing. Working through this chapter will help students to write their own evaluative texts. The chapter encourages students to begin thinking about the aims or purposes for which they are writing and then moves to the genres that typically embody those types of texts. Teachers who generally use an "aims and modes" of writing approach in their writing classes will find this organization slightly different from what they might be used to. However, starting with purposes is similar to starting with aims for writing. I then move to genres of writing rather than to modes of writing because genres are the more typical way that writing is organized throughout the various disciplines in academia. For teachers who wish to discuss modes of writing, these are included as paragraph organizational patterns in Chapter 5.

The five genres of evaluative writing covered in *Comp Online* are review, response, interpretation, synthesis, and short report. Of course, there may be other evaluative genres and some of these genres may be used for other purposes. For example, the short report may be used for informative or reflective rather than evaluative purposes. But I felt that the five genres represented here would give students a manageable introduction to evaluative writing. Each of these models was taken from actual student papers written for actual college classes.

Learning Outcomes

The learning outcomes for Chapter 8 are listed in the following chart, along with the relevant sections of the chapter and exercises that teachers can use to evaluate their students' mastery of the objectives. This chart also appears as a clickable link in the etext.

CHAPTER 8 LEARNING OUTCOMES CHART	
To assess your understanding of the Chapter 8 learning outcomes, work the corresponding You Try It exercises and study the relevant chapter sections.	
8.1 Write various types of evaluative texts.	*You Try It* 8.1.4 Write a Review Essay *You Try It* 8.2.4 Write a Response Essay *You Try It* 8.3.4 Write an Interpretive Essay *You Try It* 8.4.4 Write a Synthesis Essay *You Try It* 8.5.4 Write a Short Report
8.2 Communicate your judgment about an object or idea.	*You Try It* 8.1.4-8.5.4
8.3 Explain the criteria you are using to make that judgment.	Study Chapter 8.1-8.5

8.4 Employ good reasoning to support your evaluation.	Study Chapter 8.1-8.5

Teaching Suggestions

As you think about setting up your course syllabus, look through this chapter to see which evaluative genres you might want your students to write. These genres represent a range of difficulties, with the synthesis being perhaps the most challenging genre for students to write. Most likely, you are teaching a first-year composition course in which you will not have time to work through all of these genres with your students. However, you may be able to select one or two as an introduction to the evaluative aim or purpose.

Much of the writing that students will be asked to do in college is evaluative. So it would be a good idea to spend some time with this chapter. The *You Try It* exercises for each genre help students to take a close look at the sample paper and to think through the key features of the genre. The last *You Try It* exercise in each section (8.1–8.5) of Chapter 8 culminates in writing an evaluative text using the genre features as a generative scaffold.

Class Activities

Many of the *You Try It* exercises and assignments will be completed by students individually. However, you can also use any of the exercises as class activities. Choose the ones that you think will help your students understand the concepts in the chapter. After you have selected a genre to assign, you might want to show the video and model student paper during class using an overhead projector. Walk through the model with your students, discussing the key features of the genre with them. If you have students outline the model or write a peer review of the model, use those assignments as a springboard for class discussions about the genre.

Collaborative Activities

Have students share their responses to the *You Try It* exercises in peer pairs or in small groups. If you are teaching in an online classroom, you can use a discussion forum or chat room for collaborative activities.

Connections

Parts 1 and 2 of *Comp Online* should be taught together. That is, once you have decided which genres in Chapter 8 you are going to assign, then fold in the chapters in Part 1 that will help students to actually write in that genre. When assigning a genre from Chapter 8, I would suggest also assigning students to work through Chapter 2 in Part 1. Students will need to learn how to read critically if they are going to be successful with evaluative genres.

Use Part 3 as you would a writing handbook. That is, when you see that your students are having problems with grammar and usage, take time to guide them through the relevant sections in Part 3 that will help them correct those problems in their writing. You can individualize your instruction to have students work toward solving problems specific to their own writing.

Answers for Chapter 8 *You Try It* Exercises and Assignments

For the exercises and assignments in this chapter, answers will vary.

CHAPTER 9 / *Exploring*

MULTIMEDIA FOR CHAPTER 9

VIDEO TUTORIALS	SAMPLE DOCUMENTS	WRITING ACTIVITIES
Video 9.1 Chapter Introduction	3 Sample Exploratory Document	
Video 9.2 Exploration Model	Chart Five Exploratory Genres	*You Try It* 9.1.1 Peer Conference Advice
Video 9.3 Observation Essay	Sample Paper Observation	*You Try It* 9.1.2 Comparing the Guidelines to the Observation
	Chart Key Features of an Observation	*You Try It* 9.1.3 Practicing Outlining
	Flowchart Writing an Observation	*You Try It* 9.1.4 Write an Observation Essay
Video 9.4 Ethnographic Visual Essay	Sample Paper Ethnography	*You Try It* 9.2.1 Peer Conference Advice

	Chart Key Features of an Ethnography	*You Try It* 9.2.2 Comparing the Guidelines to the Ethnography
	Flowchart Writing an Ethnography	*You Try It* 9.2.3 Practicing Outlining
		You Try It 9.2.4 Write an Ethnography
Video 9.5 Explanatory Email	Sample Paper Explanatory Essay	*You Try It* 9.3.1 Peer Conference Advice
	Chart Key Features of an Explanation	*You Try It* 9.3.2 Comparing the Guidelines to the Explanatory Essay
	Flowchart Writing an Explanation	*You Try It* 9.3.3 Practicing Outlining
		You Try It 9.3.4 Write an Explanation
Video 9.6 Informative Email	Sample Paper Informative Essay	*You Try It* 9.4.1 Peer Conference Advice
	Chart Key Features of an Informative Essay	*You Try It* 9.4.2 Comparing the Guidelines to the Informative Essay
	Flowchart Writing an Informative Essay	*You Try It* 9.4.3 Practicing Outlining

		You Try It 9.4.4 Write an Informative Text
Video 9.7 Summary	Sample Paper Summary	You Try It 9.5.1 White Paper Response
	Chart Key Features of a Summary	You Try It 9.5.2 Practicing Outlining
	Flowchart Writing a Summary	You Try It 9.5.3 Write a Summary

Chapter Highlights

Chapter 9 introduces students to various exploratory genres of writing. Working through this chapter will help students to write their own exploratory texts. The chapter encourages students to begin thinking about the aims or purposes for which they are writing and then moves to the genres that typically embody those types of texts. Teachers who generally use an "aims and modes" of writing approach in their writing classes will find this organization slightly different from what they might be used to. However, starting with purposes is similar to starting with aims for writing. I then move to genres of writing rather than to modes of writing because genres are the more typical way that writing is organized throughout the various disciplines in academia. For teachers who wish to discuss modes of writing, these are included as paragraph organizational patterns in Chapter 5.

The five genres of exploratory writing covered in *Comp Online* are observation, ethnography, explanatory essay, informative essay, and summary. Of course, there may be other exploratory genres and some of these genres may be used for other purpose. For example, the summary may be used for evaluative or argumentative rather than exploratory purposes. But I felt that the five genres represented here would give students a manageable introduction to exploratory writing. Each of these models was taken from actual student papers written for actual college classes.

Learning Outcomes

The learning outcomes for Chapter 9 are listed in the following chart, along with the relevant sections of the chapter and exercises that teachers can use to evaluate their students' mastery of the objectives. This chart also appears as a clickable link in the etext.

CHAPTER 9 LEARNING OUTCOMES CHART	
To assess your understanding of the Chapter 9 learning outcomes, work the corresponding You Try It exercises and study the relevant chapter sections.	
9.1 Write various types of exploratory texts.	*You Try It* 9.1.4 Write an Observation Essay *You Try It* 9.2.4 Write an Ethnography *You Try It* 9.3.4 Write an Explanation *You Try It* 9.4.4 Write an Informative Text *You Try It* 9.5.4 Write a Summary
9.2 Communicate your insights about an object or idea.	*You Try It* 9.1.4-9.5.4
9.3 Explain something to readers or inform readers about what you have learned.	Study Chapter 9.3-9.4
9.4 Organize insights in an accessible way.	Study Chapter 9.1-9.5

Teaching Suggestions

As you think about setting up your course syllabus, look through this chapter to see which exploratory genres you might want your students to write. These genres represent a range of difficulties, with the ethnography being perhaps the most challenging genre for students to write because if incorporates primary research methods. Most likely you are teaching a first-year composition course in which you will not have time to work through all of these genres with your students. However, you may be able to select one or two as an introduction to the exploratory aim or purpose.

Much of the writing that students will be asked to do in college is exploratory. It would be a good idea to spend some time with this chapter. In particular, the summary is a genre that is frequently assigned across the disciplines of the academy, so that is one that you might want to assign. The *You Try It* exercises for each genre help students to take a close look at the sample paper and to think through the key features of the genre. The last *You Try It* exercise in each section (9.1–9.5) of Chapter 9 culminates in writing an exploratory text using the genre features as a generative scaffold.

Class Activities

Many of the *You Try It* exercises and assignments will be completed by students individually. However, you can also use any of the exercises as class activities. Choose the ones that you think will help your students understand the concepts in the chapter. After you have selected a genre to assign, you might want to show the video and model student paper during class using an overhead projector. Walk through the model with your students, discussing the key features of the genre with them. If you have students outline the model or write a peer review of the model, use those assignments as a springboard for class discussions about the genre.

Collaborative Activities

Have students share their responses to the *You Try It* exercises in peer pairs or in small groups. If you are teaching in an online classroom, you can use a discussion forum or chat room for collaborative activities.

Connections

Parts 1 and 2 of *Comp Online* should be taught together. That is, once you have decided which genres in Chapter 9 you are going to assign, then fold in the chapters in Part 1 that will help students to actually write in that genre. When assigning a genre from Chapter 9, I would suggest also assigning students to work through Chapters 5 and 6 in Part 1. Students will need to learn how to structure paragraphs effectively and how to revise their own work.

Use Part 3 as you would a writing handbook. That is, when you see that your students are having problems with grammar and usage, take time to guide them through the relevant sections in Part 3 that will help them correct those problems in their writing. You can individualize your instruction to have students work toward solving problems specific to their own writing.

Answers for Chapter 9 *You Try It* Exercises and Assignments

For the exercises and assignments in this chapter, answers will vary.

Chapter 10 / *Arguing*

MULTIMEDIA FOR CHAPTER 10

Video Tutorials	Sample Documents	Writing Activities
Video 10.1 Chapter Introduction	3 Sample Argument Documents	
Video 10.2 Argumentation	Chart Five Argument Genres	*You Try It* 10.1.1 Peer Conference Advice
Video 10.3 Arguing a Position	Sample Paper Arguing a Position	*You Try It* 10.1.2 Comparing the Guidelines to the Position Argument
	Chart Key Features of a Position Argument	*You Try It* 10.1.3 Practicing Outlining
	Flowchart Writing a Position Argument	*You Try It* 10.1.4 Write a Position Argument
Video 10.4 Arguing for Change	Sample Paper Arguing for Change	*You Try It* 10.2.1 Peer Conference Advice
	Chart Key Features of a Change Argument	*You Try It* 10.2.2 Comparing the Guidelines to the Change Argument

	Flowchart Writing a Change Argument	*You Try It* 10.2.3 Practicing Outlining
		You Try It 10.2.4 Write a Change Argument
Video 10.5 Critical Analysis Essay	Sample Paper Critical Analysis Essay	*You Try It* 10.3.1 Peer Conference Advice
	Chart Key Features of a Critical Analysis Essay	*You Try It* 10.3.2 Comparing the Guidelines to the Critical Analysis Essay
	Flowchart Writing a Critical Analysis Essay	*You Try It* 10.3.3 Practicing Outlining
		You Try It 10.3.4 Write a Critical Analysis
Video 10.6 Research Report	Sample Paper Research Report	*You Try It* 10.4.1 Peer Conference Advice
	Chart Key Features of a Research Report	*You Try It* 10.4.2 Comparing the Guidelines to the Research Report
	Flowchart Writing a Research Report	*You Try It* 10.4.3 Practicing Outlining
		You Try It 10.4.4 Write a Research Report

Video 10.7 Proposal	Sample Paper Proposal	*You Try It* 10.5.1 Peer Conference Advice
	Chart Key Features of a Proposal	*You Try It* 10.5.2 Comparing the Guidelines to the Proposal
	Flowchart Writing a Proposal	*You Try It* 10.5.3 Practicing Outlining
		You Try It 10.5.4 Write a Proposal

Chapter Highlights

Chapter 10 introduces students to various argumentative genres of writing. Working through this chapter will help students to write their own arguments. The chapter encourages students to begin thinking about the aims or purposes for which they are writing and then moves to the genres that typically embody those types of texts. Teachers who generally use an "aims and modes" of writing approach in their writing classes will find this organization slightly different than what they might be used to. However, starting with purposes is similar to starting with aims for writing. I then move to genres of writing rather than to modes of writing because genres are the more typical way that writing is organized throughout the various disciplines in academia. For teachers who wish to discuss modes of writing, they are included as paragraph organizational patterns in Chapter 5.

The five genres of argumentative writing covered in *Comp Online* are arguing for a position, arguing for change, critical analysis, research report, and proposal. Of course, there may be other argument genres and some of these genres may be used for other purposes. For example, the research report may be used for informative or evaluative rather than argumentative purposes. But I felt that the five genres represented here would give students a manageable introduction to argument writing. Each of these models was taken from actual student papers written for actual college classes.

Learning Outcomes

The learning outcomes for Chapter 10 are listed in the following chart, along with the relevant sections of the chapter and exercises that teachers can use to evaluate their students' mastery of the objectives. This chart also appears as a clickable link in the etext.

CHAPTER 10 LEARNING OUTCOMES CHART	
To assess your understanding of the Chapter 10 learning outcomes, work the corresponding You Try It exercises and study the relevant chapter sections.	
10.1 Write various types of argumentative texts.	*You Try It* 10.1.4 Write a Position Argument *You Try It* 10.2.4 Write a Change Argument *You Try It* 10.3.4 Write a Critical Analysis *You Try It* 10.4.4 Write a Research Report *You Try It* 10.5.4 Write a Proposal
10.2 Argue for a position or for change.	Study Chapter 10.1-10.2
10.3 Critically analyze a text or issue.	Study Chapter 10.3
10.4 Report on information you have researched.	Study Chapter 10.4
10.5 Propose a solution to a problem	Study Chapter 10.5

Teaching Suggestions

As you think about setting up your course syllabus, look through this chapter to see which argument genres you might want your students to write. Depending on how your courses are sequenced, you may or may not want to spend much time on argument with your class. If you are teaching a first semester course and students will then take a second-semester course whose focus is argumentation, you may want to just briefly introduce these genres in the first-semester course. Perhaps you can have students write an arguing-for-change letter or memo, for example, as an introduction to argumentation, without assigning a full-blown research report or critical essay.

These genres represent a range of difficulties, with the research report being perhaps the most challenging genre for students to write. Most likely you are teaching a first-year composition course in which you will not have time to work through all of these genres with your students. However, you may be able to select one or two as an introduction to the argument aim or purpose.

Much of the writing that students will be asked to do in college is argumentative. So it would be a good idea to spend at least some time with this chapter. In particular, the research report is a genre that is frequently assigned across the disciplines of the academy, so that is one that you might want to consider assigning. The *You Try It* exercises for each genre help students to take a close look at the sample paper and to think through the key features of the genre. The last *You Try It* exercise in each section (10.1–10.5) of Chapter 10 culminates in writing an argumentative text using the genre features as a generative scaffold.

Class Activities

Many of the *You Try It* exercises and assignments will be completed by students individually. However, you can also use any of the exercises as class activities. Choose the ones that you think will help your students understand the concepts in the chapter. After you have selected a genre to assign, you might want to show the video and model student paper during class using an overhead projector. Walk through the model with your students, discussing the key features of the genre with them. If you have students outline the model or write a peer review of the model, use those assignments as a springboard for class discussions about the genre.

Collaborative Activities

Have students share their responses to the *You Try It* exercises in peer pairs or in small groups. If you are teaching in an online classroom, you can use a discussion forum or chat room for collaborative activities.

Connections

Parts 1 and 2 of *Comp Online* should be taught together. That is, once you have decided which genres in Chapter 10 you are going to assign, then fold in the chapters in Part 1 that will help students to actually write in that genre. When assigning a genre from Chapter 10, I would suggest also assigning students to work through Chapter 4 in Part 1. Students will need to learn how to formulate their own arguments appropriately and how to avoid logical fallacies as they work to build a compelling case.

Use Part 3 as you would a writing handbook. That is, when you see that your students are having problems with grammar and usage, take time to guide them through the relevant sections in Part 3 that will help them correct those problems in their writing. You can individualize your instruction to have students work toward solving problems specific to their own writing.

Answers for Chapter 10 *You Try It* Exercises and Assignments

For the exercises and assignments in this chapter, answers will vary.

PART**THREE**

Editing and Proofreading

CHAPTER 11 / *Sentences*

MULTIMEDIA FOR CHAPTER 11

VIDEO TUTORIALS	SAMPLE DOCUMENTS	WRITING ACTIVITIES
Video 11.1 Chapter Introduction	Chart Types of Nouns and Their Roles	*You Try It* 11.1 Fixing Fragments
Video 11.2 Using Spelling-, Style-, and Grammar-, Checkers	Chart Types of Pronouns and Their Roles	*You Try It* 11.2 Fixing Comma Splices and Run-On Sentences
Video 11.3 Pronoun Case Problems	Chart Verb Tenses	*You Try It* 11.3 Correcting Pronoun Errors
Video 11.4 Wrong Verb Tense or Form	Chart Common Prepositions	*You Try It* 11.4 Pronoun Agreement
Video 11.5 Adjective/Adverb Confusion	Chart Some Common Subordinating Conjunctions	*You Try It* 11.5 Subject-Verb Agreement

Video 11.6 Preposition Problems	Checklist Fixing Fragments	*You Try It* 11.6 Correcting Modifier Errors
Video 11.7 Parallelism	Common Errors Pronoun Reference	*You Try It* 11.7 Correcting Shifts in Tense and Tone
Video 11.8 Recognizing Sentence Fragments	Common Errors Subject-Verb Agreement	*You Try It* 11.8 Correcting Mixed Constructions
Video 11.9 Sentence Fragments	Common Errors Clarity and Conciseness	*You Try It* 11.9 Revising Sentences for Clarity and Conciseness
Video 11.10 Fused (Run-on) Sentences	Chart Wordy and Concise Phrases	*You Try It* 11.10 Revising Wordy Sentences
Video 11.11 Pronoun Reference Problems		*You Try It* 11.11 Revising Noun-Heavy Sentences
Video 11.12 Lack of Pronoun- Antecedent Agreement		
Video 11.13 Recognizing Pronoun Problems		
Video 11.14 How to Recognize Subject-Verb Problems		

Video 11.15 Subject-Verb Agreement		
Video 11.16 Dangling and Misplaced Modifiers		
Video 11.17 Faulty Shifts in Tense		
Video 11.18 Wordiness and Redundancy		

Chapter Highlights

This chapter presents an overview of basic sentence structure as well as suggestions for how to recognize and correct common sentence problems and how to edit sentences for clarity and style. It will be useful both for students who have never studied English grammar and style, and for students who need a quick review. Topics include parts of speech, basic sentence patterns, common sentence-level errors, and editing advice. The chapter introduces many grammatical terms that students need to understand in order to make full use of other chapters in Part 3. These terms are also included in the glossary.

Learning Outcomes

The learning outcomes for Chapter 11 are listed in the following below, along with the relevant sections of the chapter and exercises that teachers can use to evaluate their students' mastery of the objectives. This chart also appears as a clickable link in the etext.

Chapter 11 Learning Outcomes Chart	
To assess your understanding of the Chapter 11 learning outcomes, work the corresponding You Try It exercises and study the relevant chapter sections.	
11.1 Understand the basic elements of sentence structure.	Study Chapter 11.1
11.2 Recognize and correct common sentence problems.	*You Try It* 11.1, 11.2, 11.3, 11.4, 11.5, 11.6, 11.7, 11.8
11.3 Edit sentences for clarity and style.	Study Chapter 11.8 *You Try It* 11.9 Revising Sentences for Clarity and Conciseness *You Try It* 11.10 Revising Wordy Sentences *You Try It* 11.11 Revising Noun-Heavy Sentences

Teaching Suggestions

This nuts-and-bolts material is unlikely to engage the attention of students for very long. Instead of spending a lot of class time on the chapter, you may prefer to assign it as homework, familiarizing students with its content so that they can return to it as needed when working on their writing assignments. As you discover specific sentence-level problems in your students' writing, you can key in on sections of this chapter that will help students correct these common errors in their own work.

Computer Activities

Many students are likely to have access to a style/grammar checker. Some may use it properly, others may use it ineffectively, and still others may not use it at all. We suggest you take time at this early stage of style/grammar instruction to show the latter two groups how to use a style/grammar checker. Find a paragraph-length text and run the checker on it. If you have a computerized classroom, you can do this in class; if not, you will have to do it before class and show students a marked-up hard copy. Encourage all your students to view Video 11.2 to review the features of spelling-, style-, and grammar-checkers.

11.1 Understand the basic elements of sentence structure

Class Activities

Have a student write a sentence on the black- or whiteboard (perhaps from one of his or her own writings), and then have the class identify what part of speech each word is. If the sentence is too simple, solicit a second, more complex one.

Teaching Suggestions

Students need to know how to identify the simple subject (11.1b) in order to determine number agreement. Also, they need to be able to distinguish between the subject and the predicate in order to make stylistic adjustments, such as switching between active and passive voice. It would be a good idea to spend some time on this section of the chapter with your class.

Another reason to understand basic sentence structure is to keep grammatical elements balanced or in the same form, e.g., parallelism. This concept will help your students to revise their sentences for readability.

11.2 Sentence fragments

Chapter Highlights

This section of the chapter covers a persistent problem for many student writers—the grammatically incomplete sentence, or sentence fragment. It tells students how to guard against producing fragments, and it provides

101

specific suggestions for fixing fragments. The chapter also gives cautious encouragement and advice on using a style/grammar checker to identify fragments.

Teaching Suggestions

Most fragments in student writing are a result of improper punctuation. As you work through this chapter with your class, look for opportunities to direct students' attention to appropriate sections of Chapter 13, Punctuation.

Computer Activities

Have students use the word processor to locate fragments in their own writing or in a flawed text that you have located or prepared for them. Remind students that customizing the style/grammar checker will help them find what they're looking for more quickly. (Note: Sentence fragments are sometimes listed under CLAUSE ERRORS.) Have students fix all fragments they find, using the Checklist for Fixing Fragments in Chapter 11.2c.

ESL Note

Some languages do not require an overt subject in declarative sentences. In Spanish, for example, subject pronouns are often omitted. Consider the following example:

> A book is like a piece of rope. Takes on meaning only in connection with the things it holds together.

Translated directly into Spanish, it would be grammatically correct. If your Spanish-speaking students omit subject pronouns when speaking or writing in English, it may be because of first-language interference.

Teaching Suggestions

Students are often exposed to fragments in advertisements, cartoons, signs, and other forms of public discourse, as well as in certain literary forms such as poems and plays. Emphasize to students that formal writing differs from these other genres in that it does not tolerate sentence fragments to the same degree, if at all.

11.3 Comma splices and run-on sentences

Chapter Highlights

This section of the chapter discusses two common errors in student writing—comma splices and run-on sentences. After describing these problems, the chapter suggests four different ways to correct them.

Teaching Suggestions

Comma splices and run-on sentences result from incorrect punctuation. We suggest, therefore, that you link your instruction in this chapter to instruction in punctuation (Chapter 13).

ESL Note

Comma splices are acceptable in formal German, Dutch, and many other languages.

11.4 Pronoun reference and agreement

Chapter Highlights

Pronouns can make writing more concise and readable, but they can also cause confusion. This section of the chapter discusses some of the main problems that student writers have with pronouns—lack of a specific antecedent, pronoun-antecedent agreement, overly broad reference, mixed use of *it*, and inconsistent use of *that*, *which*, and *who*—and includes specific guidelines for preventing these problems.

Teaching Suggestions

Many of the pronoun problems described in this chapter occur because students incorporate a conversational style in their writing. Colloquial English often uses vague pronouns like those illustrated in Chapter 11.4a— for example, "*They* say that . . ." Since these problems are most likely to crop up in students' unedited writing, we suggest the following exercise: In a sample of writing that they did quickly, such as a rough draft, freewriting, or a placement essay, have students underline all pronouns and determine whether they adhere to the guidelines presented in the chapter.

Computer Activities

Have students do the exercise just described with the aid of their word processing program's search function.

Teaching Suggestions

Colloquial speech often mixes up pronouns and their antecedents, but students need to understand how to correct those errors when writing. This section outlines common errors and the rules students need to know to avoid them.

Teaching Suggestions

Using *it*, *that*, *which*, and *this* too often produces not only referential confusion but also an irritating stylistic repetitiveness. Stress to students that good writers take care to avoid such repetition.

Computer Novice Notes

Style/grammar checkers typically contain a rule requiring writers to use *that*, not *which*, in essential relative clauses. As noted in the text, however, many expert writers use either *that* or *which*, depending on rhetorical and aesthetic considerations. Use this opportunity to point out to students how the information in style/grammar checkers is often oversimplified.

Teaching Suggestions

Many students find it difficult to get around the sexist pronoun problem in a way that is not awkward. Explain that expert writers use not just one but a variety of techniques to deal with this thorny issue. Refer them to the extended discussion of how to avoid biased language in Chapter 12.

11.5 Subject-verb agreement

Chapter Highlights

This section of the chapter discusses grammatical agreement, or concord, between subjects and verbs. In English, the two major forms of agreement are that between subject and verb and that between pronoun and antecedent (see Chapter 11.4). The discussion of subject-verb agreement focuses largely on whether certain kinds of subjects are singular or plural. The examples address agreement in varying subject-verb circumstances.

Teaching Suggestions

If particular students are having problems with subject-verb agreement, be sure to have them review the videos and work the *You Try It* exercise provided in this section of the chapter.

11.6 **Misplaced and dangling modifiers**

Chapter Highlights

This section of the chapter is designed to help students avoid common errors in the use of modifiers. It offers five guidelines to promote clarity and readability: position modifiers close to the words they modify, avoid ambiguity, try to put lengthy modifiers at the beginning or end, avoid disruptive modifiers, and avoid dangling modifiers.

Teaching Suggestions

If students are unsure about what a modifier is and how it is used, have them review the videos and work the *You Try It* exercise provided in this section of the chapter.

Connections

The funnier examples in this chapter are taken from Richard Lederer's *Anguished English* (New York: Wyrick, 1987). We highly recommend this book as a source of humor for all writing teachers and students.

Computer Novice Notes

Ordinary style/grammar checkers cannot identify misplaced or dangling modifiers.

Linguistic Note

The split infinitive became an object of attention only fairly recently in the history of English stylistics. It was in the nineteenth century that certain pedants began to claim that, because Latin infinitives cannot be split (since they are written as single words), English infinitives should not be split either. But all languages have their own internal logic, and it is a mistake to impose the logic of one language on another.

11.7 **Faulty shifts**

Chapter Highlights

Sometimes students' writing tends to skip from one time frame to another or from one topic to another, for no apparent reason. This section of the chapter advises writers to maintain consistency in their writing, specifically by avoiding unnecessary shifts in person and number; avoiding unnecessary shifts in verb tense, mood, and subject; avoiding shifts in tone; avoiding mixed constructions; and creating consistency between subjects and predicates.

Teaching Suggestions

"A foolish consistency is the hobgoblin of little minds" (Ralph Waldo Emerson, *Essays: Self-Reliance*). If it is overdone, consistency can drain writing of its variety and vitality. Show students a page of prose by a well-known author that contains appropriate shifts of tense, mood, and subject. Discuss with them the possible reasons behind such shifts. When reviewing the chapter, emphasize to students that the guidelines given are meant to guard against *unnecessary* shifts, not against rhetorically appropriate ones.

Class Activities

Review all the guidelines in this chapter. Then have students pair off and examine samples of their own writing for errors of consistency. This activity can be done online in a discussion forum or chat room.

11.8 **Clarity and conciseness**

Chapter Highlights

This section of the chapter covers a number of strategies for making writing clearer and more concise: avoiding excessively long sentences and unnecessary repetition and redundancy, using expletives and passive-voice sentences only where necessary, eliminating wordy phrases, and avoiding a noun-heavy style.

Computer Activities

Have students set a maximum sentence length on their grammar checker. Then have them test a sample of their writing.

Connections

Excessively long sentences can result from improper punctuation creating comma splices or run-on sentences (see also Chapter 13 on punctuation).

ESL Note

Excessive repetition is a problem for all but the most advanced ESL students. When learning a second language, students tend to settle on a safe, basic vocabulary and do not learn enough synonyms. Encourage students to develop secondary vocabulary.

Teaching Suggestions

Most writing that has not been carefully scrutinized by a professional editor contains some wordiness. Look for examples in your local environment— for example, in the campus newspaper or in junk mail—and have students do the same. You may even want to compile a set of "prize-winning" examples or a list of wordy expressions for future use.

Class Activities

Put a short, simple sentence on the board and have students deliberately create a wordy paraphrase of it. This activity can be very amusing, especially if you make it competitive by seeing who can use the most words. You could also do this activity online in a discussion forum or chat room.

Answers for Chapter 11 *You Try It* Exercises

➲ *You Try It* 11.1 Fixing Fragments

1. John Lennon was killed in 1980 by a deranged young man.
2. Were it not for the dynamics of racism in U.S. society, Chuck Berry probably would have been crowned king of rock and roll.
3. It was the phenomenal success of "Rapper's Delight" that first alerted the mainstream media to the existence of hip-hop.

4. Barry Bonds hit seventy-three home runs in one year, setting a new record.

5. Mauritania is an Islamic country that is located in northwest Africa.

6. Lamarck thought that acquired traits could be passed on to one's offspring. His ideas were challenged much later by Charles Darwin.

7. Having thought about our situation, I have decided I should take a second job.

8. This is a good economic arrangement for working and taking care of the children.

9. Two years after his disastrous invasion of Russia in 1812, Napoleon was exiled to the island of Elba.

10. He regained power the following year but was defeated at Waterloo.

➲ *You Try It* 11.2 Fixing Comma Splices and Run-On Sentences

1. Ritchie Valens was the first Chicano rock and roll star. He recorded a string of hits before his fatal plane crash in February 1959.

2. In order to access the Internet via modem you must install the Dial-Up Networking option. Click here to start.

3. I started reading Russian literature when I was young, though I did not know that it was Russian; in fact I was not even aware that I lived in a country with any distinct existence of its own.

4. We always ate dinner at eight o'clock. We spent the whole day anticipating the time we could talk and eat together as a family.

5. Mine is a Spanish-speaking household; we use Spanish exclusively.

6. The side pockets of her jacket were always bulging. They were filled with rocks, candy, chewing gum, and other trinkets only a child could appreciate.

7. Some people seem to be able to eat everything they want, yet they do not gain weight.

8. The VCR was not a popular piece of equipment with movie moguls, but the studios quickly adapted.

9. Some magazines survive without advertising; they are supported by readers who pay for subscriptions.

10. A multimillion-dollar diet industry has developed, which sells liquid diets, freeze-dried foods, artificial sweeteners, and diet books by the hundreds.

➲ *You Try It* 11.3 Correcting Pronoun Errors

1. *Sesame Street* is a valuable children's program. Not only are you able to learn from a show like this, you also are able to fall in love with your favorite character, who has the ability to become your friend and teacher.
2. Then there is the Disney book club, which provides short-story versions of the animated films.
3. The sentence is correct as is.
4. We do not tear your clothing with machinery. We clean it carefully by hand.
5. You should bring your book to class tomorrow and be prepared to discuss Chapter 6. It is important for you to do this.
6. Only one of the members of the House of Representatives decided that he would vote against the proposed bill.
7. Experts say that drinking and driving kills more people each year than cancer. One should not drink and drive.
8. Filling out college applications and worrying about SAT scores are annual rituals for many high school seniors. They are a part of the admissions process.
9. The annual report says it has been a disappointing year for the company.
10. The dog that chases my cat lives in the house across the street. [*That* is better, given the informality of the sentence and the euphony.]

⊃ *You Try It* 11.4 Pronoun Agreement

1. **Earthquakes** most often occur near a fault line, and *they* are usually impossible to predict.

2. **Tony** and **Michiyo** are here to pick up *their* final research projects.

3. Some of the **coaches** have lost *their* faith in the team.

4. Drinking and driving can cause fatal automobile **accidents**, but *they* can easily be prevented.

5. **Everything** in the office was in *its* proper place.

6. The **members** of the committee took three hours to make *their* decision.

7. Choong was required to take **physics** during his undergraduate course of study, and he was sure that *it* would be a very difficult subject.

8. The **NBA** imposes fines on *its* athletes if they break the rules.

9. Neither the former owners nor the current **owner** could find *his* signature on any of the documents.

10. A **lawyer** should always treat *his or her* clients with respect.

⊃ *You Try It* 11.5 Subject-verb Agreement

1. The clocks in this building *run* slow.

2. Basketball and football *are* Lucy's favorite sports.

3. Either my brother or my cousins *are* coming to babysit the children.

4. Neither my sisters nor Todd *is* interested in going to college.

5. Each of the Spanish club members *is* going to bring an authentic Hispanic dish to share.

6. All of the Norwegians studying in the United States *celebrate* Norwegian Independence Day on May 17.

7. All of her love *was* manifest in the poem she wrote him.

8. The faculty of the English department *decides* how many fellowships are granted each year.

9. Many Americans believe that White House politics *are* corrupt. [This sentence assumes that politics refers to political activities; if it referred instead to political life or the field of international politics, *is* would be correct.]

10. There *are* several different dresses you can try on that are in your size.

⊃ *You Try It* 11.6 Correcting Modifier Errors

1. Politicians who frequently run for office need to raise a lot of money.
2. The Groveton police reported two cars stolen yesterday.
3. To get the job, he had to completely revise his résumé.
4. Please take time to look over the brochure with photos of your family that is enclosed.
5. Before installing a new program, you should turn off all other applications.
6. Because Melissa missed class four times in three weeks, Professor Kateb decided that she should be penalized.
7. In an interview with Barbara Walters, Yoko Ono will talk about her husband, John Lennon, who was killed.
8. The patient with a severe emotional problem was referred to a psychiatrist.
9. In a New Hampshire court, a former scout leader will plead guilty to two counts of sexually assaulting two boys.
10. For the second time, the judge sentenced the killer to die in the electric chair.

⊃ *You Try It* 11.7 Correcting Shifts in Tense and Tone

1. One should do some type of physical activity at least three times a week for thirty minutes. Regular exercise is good for one's heart and lungs.
2. We wanted to go to the U2 concert. However, the tickets sold out before we even got there, and there was no chance that we could buy them from scalpers for less than $100.
3. Those who do not love themselves can never hope to love anyone else.
4. We hike up in the mountains every Saturday morning. We love the feeling of sheer exhilaration. We are happy to be tired.
5. Elizabeth Bishop's "First Death in Nova Scotia" discusses death from the point of view of a child. It paints a picture of a young girl's emotional reaction to the death of her cousin.
6. If she were rich, she would buy all her clothes at Nordstrom and Lord and Taylor.
7. If you want to learn to speed-read, you have to first learn to concentrate. You need to focus on the words on the page. It is

important not to let your attention wander. Your eyes should always catch the center of each page.

8. If our goal is educational and economic equity and parity, then we need affirmative action to correct the lingering effects of prejudice. We are behind as a result of discrimination and denial of opportunity, and that is completely unfair.

9. Married couples make a commitment to each other and to society; in exchange, society extends certain benefits to them, which helps them out financially and in other ways.

10. There can be no excuse for what you did. The act is shameful, and you should not be forgiven for it.

➲ *You Try It* 11.8 Correcting Mixed Constructions

Answers will vary. Following are some possible answers.

1. Using the terms *alligator* and *crocodile* to refer to the same reptile misleads many people.
2. A foot is equivalent to twelve inches.
3. The job of all UPS drivers is to deliver packages from their cities of origin to their final destinations.
4. She asked if you liked the concert.
5. The Slavic Festival was so popular, in part, because it had a band that played polka music.
6. Creative writers, such as Lita, romanticize their adventures.
7. Strawberries are picked while slightly green because, if left to ripen, they would rot before they were picked.
8. When the homecoming parade included William Smith and Ted Jackson, they became school heroes.
9. Processing caramels at high heat softens their centers.
10. The Great Salt Lake is easy to swim in because of its high salt content, which makes the water more buoyant.

➲*You Try It* 11.9 Revising Sentences for Clarity and Conciseness

1. Millions of people witnessed the first landing on the moon.
2. She did the daily paperwork.
3. I had a frightening experience when my teenage daughter took me out for a drive.
4. The quarterback had been injured early in the season and had undergone extensive knee surgery to repair the damage. He had

been conscientious about his rehabilitation exercises and was therefore ready to play again only four months after the surgery.

5. Because the trumpeter lacked warm mittens and a hat on that very cold morning, she was unable to play well during the halftime show at the Thanksgiving game.

6. The Girl Scouts sang several unusual songs during their annual awards ceremony.

7. A boy who works with my son during the summer achieved the Boy Scout Eagle rank.

8. Hundreds of items were marked down for the annual August clearance sale.

9. Many people in this society do not have enough leisure time.

10. Students often find their work piling up during finals.

⊃ *You Try It* 11.10 Revising Wordy Sentences

1. *sample exercise*
2. summarize
3. emphasize
4. operate on
5. analyze
6. estimate
7. realize
8. explain
9. sympathize with
10. inspect

⊃ *You Try It* 11.11 Revising Noun-Heavy Sentences

1. The scientist concluded that she had made an important discovery.

2. The United Nations wanted to inspect the country's weapons storage facilities.

3. The committee decided to hire the man it had interviewed.

4. The institution's stance on affirmative action was unclear.

5. The group believed that disaster was coming at the close of the century.

6. My mechanic thinks there is nothing wrong with my car's transmission.

7. Their press release explained the demonstrators' behavior.

8. The education reform law passed by the legislature demands that schools improve their ways of teaching.

9. The music theory course requires composing a piece of music.
10. The man was justifiably proud of having achieved his goal.

CHAPTER 12 / *Words*

MULTIMEDIA FOR CHAPTER 12

VIDEO TUTORIALS	SAMPLE DOCUMENTS	WRITING ACTIVITIES
Video 12.1 Chapter Introduction	Chart Common Errors: Choosing Words	*You Try It* 12.1 General Versus Specific Words
Video 12.2 Using Appropriate Language	Chart Sexist and Gender Neutral Nouns	*You Try It* 12.2 Synonyms and Connotation
Video 12.3 Varieties of English	Guidelines Avoiding the Generic Pronoun Problem	*You Try It* 12.3 Formal and Informal Language
Video 12.4 Using Inclusive Language		*You Try It* 12.4 Translating Jargon and Slang
		You Try It 12.5 Revising Pretentious Language
		You Try It 12.6 Removing Biased Language
		You Try It 12.7 Revising Biased Language

Chapter Highlights

Words are the brickwork of writing, the basic elements that convey meaning. This chapter covers some of the most important dimensions of word choice: denotation, connotation, level of formality, jargon, and pretentiousness. The chapter also covers ways to avoid biased language and gender references.

Learning Outcomes

The learning outcomes for Chapter 12 are listed in the chart below, along with the relevant sections of the chapter and exercises that teachers can use to evaluate their students' mastery of the objectives. This chart also appears as a clickable link in the etext.

CHAPTER 12 LEARNING OUTCOMES CHART	
To assess your understanding of the Chapter 12 learning outcomes, work the corresponding You Try It exercises and study the relevant chapter sections.	
12.1 Choose words that have the right meaning, connotation, and level of formality.	*You Try It* 12.1 General Versus Specific Words *You Try It* 12.2 Synonyms and Connotation *You Try It* 12.3 Formal and Informal Language
12.2 Understand and avoid jargon, slang, and pretentious language.	*You Try It* 12.4 Translating Jargon and Slang *You Try It* 12.5 Revising Pretentious Language

12.3 Avoid biased language and gender references.	*You Try It* 12.6 Removing Biased Language
	You Try It 12.7 Revising Biased Language

Teaching Suggestions

Students often do not realize the impact of choosing the right word to effectively convey their message. Use this chapter to heighten students' awareness of the need to revise not only at the sentence level, but also at the word level.

In working through this chapter, students will benefit greatly from using a dictionary and a thesaurus. Familiarize them with online dictionaries and thesauruses that they may wish to use while revising and editing their own writing.

12.1 **Choosing the right words**

Class Activities

1. Find a well-written paragraph and retype it, making some of its key words more general or more specific, more concrete or more abstract. Then challenge students to identify the changes you have made and guess what the original words were. This activity may be done online in a discussion forum or chat room.

2. Find a short, well-written letter to the editor that has two or more connotative words. Retype the letter, blanking out those particular words. Then, using a thesaurus, find two synonyms for each of those words that differ slightly in their connotations. Present the letter to your students along with the three possible words (the original word plus two synonyms) for each blank, and challenge them to select the best one (which may or may not be the original). This activity can lead to lively class discussion! This activity may be done online in a discussion forum or chat room.

12.2 Avoiding jargon, slang, and pretentiousness

Class Activities

Almost everyone has a special interest (for example, a sport or a hobby) that involves some use of jargon. Ask students to write a jargon-filled sentence, drawing on one of their special interests. Have them read their sentences aloud and let the other students try to guess what the terms mean. Then have all the students rewrite their sentences in "plain English" (perhaps working in groups of two or three). This activity should sensitize students to the exclusionary power of jargon. This activity may be done online in a discussion forum or chat room.

12.3 Avoiding biased and sexist language

Chapter Highlights

This section of the chapter begins with the premise that "language is arguably the single most powerful tool we humans have." It notes that our use of language must conform to certain conventions yet be flexible enough to enable linguistic creativity. This section deals with bias in language, including gender discrimination, racial/ethnic discrimination, age discrimination, and other sociological differences.

ESL Note

Bias can be evident in any language, not just English. Have ESL students reflect on their native language and how it may sometimes be used in a biased way.

Class Activities

1. Have students look for and record examples of the use of biased language in the public domain. Some possible sources include radio and TV talk shows, letters to the editor, and Internet chat groups. This activity may be done online in a discussion forum or chat room.

2. When Dr. Benjamin Spock first published his famous baby book, *The Common Sense Book of Baby and Child Care*, in 1945, there was little or no public consciousness of gender discrimination in language. Accordingly, when Dr. Spock needed to use a pronoun to refer to a

baby, he used the generic *he*. He continued this practice in the 1968 edition of the book, as in this sentence about diapering: "Most mothers change the diapers when they pick the baby up for his feeding and again before they put him back to bed" (p. 175). By 1976, however, he had come to realize the prejudicial nature of this practice, and so he published a newly revised edition, which includes this prefatory comment: "The main reason for this 3rd revision (4th edition) of *Baby and Child Care* is to eliminate the sexist biases of the sort that help to create and perpetuate discrimination against girls and women. Earlier editions referred to the child of indeterminate sex as he. Though this in one sense is only a literary tradition, it, like many other traditions, implies that the masculine sex has some kind of priority" (p. xix).

Have students try to guess how Dr. Spock revised the 1968 sentence about diapering for the 1976 edition of his book. [Answer: "Most parents change the diapers when they pick the baby up for feeding and again before they put the child back to bed" (pp. 207–208).] Once you have told students the 1976 version of the sentence, discuss all the changes Dr. Spock made. This activity may be done in a discussion forum.

3. There has been much public debate in recent years about the appropriateness of using ethnic names for sports teams, the most publicized example being the Washington Redskins football team. Have a brief class discussion about this issue, making a point to raise more questions than answers. If there are students who do not object to the name Washington Redskins, you might ask whether they would object to the name Washington Honkies or Washington Rednecks. After a short discussion period, have students write a short essay expressing and supporting their point of view. This activity may be done in a discussion forum.

4. We have provided only a few of the many examples that exist of biased language about age and other differences. Have students think of other examples and write a brief analysis of them. This activity may be done online in a discussion forum or chat room.

Answers for Chapter 12 *You Try It* Exercises

➲ *You Try It* 12.1 General Versus Specific Words

Answers will vary. Following are some possible answers.

1. *sample exercise*
2. pollution, air pollution, smog, urban smog, dense urban smog
3. decoration, interior decoration, plants, potted plants, ferns
4. building, dwelling, cabin, log cabin, old log cabin
5. organism, animal, grazing animal, cow, Guernsey cow
6. material, building material, wood, hardwood, oak
7. food, main dish, casserole, rice casserole, shrimp creole
8. recreational activity, sport, racquet sport, tennis, mixed-doubles tennis
9. clothing, garment, suit, men's suit, tuxedo
10. ritual, ceremony, religious ceremony, baptism, baptism by immersion

➲ *You Try It* 12.2 Synonyms and Connotation

Answers may vary, depending on the context. Potential variations are a good topic for class discussion.

1. bright, smart, intelligent, apt, clever, shrewd
2. slim, slender, lanky, thin, skinny, gaunt
3. dynamic, assertive, forceful, aggressive, pushy, domineering
4. humorous, funny, amusing, silly, comical, ridiculous
5. broke, insolvent, poor, penniless, indigent, destitute
6. circle, clan, faction, clique, gang
7. self-reliant, independent, autonomous, separate, solitary
8. innocent, childlike, callow, green, immature
9. unbroken, untamed, wild, animalistic, bestial
10. disheveled, untidy, messy, unkempt, sloppy

➲ *You Try It* 12.3 Formal and Informal Language

1. If you find any flaws in the program, please tell me.
2. Ahab was so obsessed with locating the white whale, he went insane.

3. When the savings and loans started failing in the 1980s, many small investors found themselves in desperate trouble.
4. At present, good workers are hard to find.
5. Too often social workers are blamed for all the ills of the welfare system.
6. My neighbor was duped by a swindler selling vinyl siding.
7. My younger brother is an apprentice mechanic at the garage downtown.
8. The food at the new restaurant is inexpensive, but it tastes good.
9. Customers should not have to tolerate poor service.
10. I am angry about government waste.

➲ *You Try It* 12.4 Translating Jargon and Slang

Answers will vary.

➲ *You Try It* 12.5 Revising Pretentious Language

1. Where there's smoke, there's fire.
2. Two heads are better than one.
3. Birds of a feather flock together.
4. The more things change, the more they stay the same.
5. The acorn does not fall far from the tree.
6. No matter where you go, there you are.
7. You are barking up the wrong tree.
8. A stitch in time saves nine.
9. People who live in glass houses shouldn't throw stones.
10. Don't cry over spilt milk.

➲ *You Try It* 12.6 Removing Biased Language

1. The newly revised cookbook would be a welcome addition to anyone's library.
2. Some Asian Americans are good at math.
3. A professional nurse has a responsibility to keep up with developments in his or her field [or in the field].
4. The man has unconventional ideas!
5. The church held a food drive to make sure that no children went hungry.
6. We await the day when someone discovers a cure for the common cold.

7. Some older people need help taking care of themselves.
8. The physical education teacher told the two boys not to speak Spanish in her class.
9. We must pay attention to the needs of deaf people and aphonic people.
10. The shrewd businessman made a handsome profit.

➲ *You Try It* 12.7 Revising Biased Language

Answers will vary. Following is a possible answer.

The dominance of the Anglo-American culture placed great pressure on immigrants to blend into the mainstream way of life. The children of most immigrants dropped their distinctive customs and native language more quickly than their elders, assuming the culture and language of English-speaking Americans. In fact, just a few short years after their grandparents had arrived from Europe, the grandchildren of immigrants had embraced a new American identity and way of life.

Chapter 13 / *Punctuation*

MULTIMEDIA FOR CHAPTER 13

VIDEO TUTORIALS	SAMPLE DOCUMENTS	WRITING ACTIVITIES
Video 13.1 Chapter Introduction	Chart Common Errors: Apostrophes	*You Try It* 13.1 Correcting Punctuation Errors
Video 13.2 Comma Problems and Word Processing	Chart Common Errors: Quotation Marks	*You Try It* 13.2 Adding End Punctuation
Video 13.3 Missing or Unnecessary Commas		*You Try It* 13.3 Correcting Comma Errors
Video 13.5 Misusing the Apostrophe		*You Try It* 13.4 Correcting Comma Errors
Video 13.6 Misusing the Apostrophe		*You Try It* 13.5 Correcting Comma Errors
		You Try It 13.6 Removing Unnecessary Commas
		You Try It 13.7 Correcting Punctuation Errors

		You Try It 13.8 Correcting Apostrophe Errors

Chapter Highlights

Many students are uncertain about how to punctuate abbreviations, indirect questions, and quotations; they use periods instead of commas to mark pauses and overuse exclamation points. This chapter is designed to help those students. It covers avoiding common misuses of commas and other punctuation marks as well as provides advice for editing punctuation.

Learning Outcomes

The learning outcomes for Chapter 13 are listed in the chart below, along with the relevant sections of the chapter and exercises that teachers can use to evaluate their students' mastery of the objectives. This chart also appears as a clickable link in the etext.

CHAPTER 13 LEARNING OUTCOMES CHART	
To assess your understanding of the Chapter 13 learning outcomes, work the corresponding You Try It exercises and study the relevant chapter sections.	
13.1 Avoid common misuses of commas and other punctuation marks.	*You Try It* 13.1 Correcting Punctuation Errors *You Try It* 13.2 Adding End Punctuation *You Try It* 13.3 Correcting Comma Errors *You Try It* 13.4 Correcting Comma Errors *You Try It* 13.5 Correcting Comma Errors

	You Try It 13.7 Correcting Punctuation Errors *You Try It* 13.8 Correcting Apostrophe Errors
13.2 Edit your writing to use punctuation correctly and clearly.	*You Try It* 13.6 Removing Unnecessary Commas

13.1 **The period**

Connections

To teach students not to use periods to mark pauses, have them review Chapter 11.2 on Sentence Fragments. To help them avoid comma splices and run-on sentences, have them review Chapter 11.3.

13.2 **The question mark**

Teaching Suggestions

Have students practice using question marks for direct address with quotation marks. Punctuating quotations is often confusing for students.

13.3 **The exclamation point**

Teaching Suggestions

Remind students that exclamation points are frequently overused. Ask them to bring to class (or post online) examples of excessive use of exclamation points that they have run across in their reading.

13.4 **The comma**

Chapter Highlights

The comma is arguably the most important—and challenging to use—punctuation mark in the English language. Thus, it is worth spending as much class time as possible on it. This section of the chapter describes virtually all of the comma's uses, from setting off introductory phrases or clauses to setting off markers of direct address. You may want to remind students to revisit this information from time to time.

Class Activities

Collect students' sentences containing comma errors. From time to time, show these sentences to the class on an overhead transparency or handout and have students make the appropriate corrections. This activity may also be done online in a discussion forum or chat room.

Teaching Suggestions

Students may argue that a comma is needed only after long introductory elements, not after shorter ones. They may even cite authors who follow this practice. Our response to these students is to ask them, "Where do you draw the line between 'long' and 'short'?" Professional authors have a good sense of where to draw the line in any particular case, but students generally do not. By having them put a comma after all introductory elements beyond single words, you relieve them of the guesswork.

Linguistic Note

What kind of punctuation mark you should use when combining sentences depends, in part, on how strong you want the connection to be. A good discussion of this issue can be found in J. Dawkins, "Teaching Punctuation as a Rhetorical Tool," *College Composition and Communication* 46.4 (December 1995).

Connections

As noted in the text, conjunctive adverbs are important transitional devices, serving as "traffic signals" for the reader. Their role as a transitional device is especially noticeable in paragraphs, so we suggest that you have students review Chapter 5.3, on using transitional words and phrases to link sentences.

13.5 The semicolon

Chapter Highlights

The semicolon is perhaps the least understood of all punctuation marks. Many students are so mystified by semicolons that they avoid them at all costs. This is unfortunate, because the semicolon has several important uses, which this section of the chapter describes. It also warns against some common misuses.

Teaching Suggestions

While many students do not use semicolons at all, others use them to excess. They may routinely use a semicolon in every sentence that contains more than one clause. Be on the alert for this habit, and have all students aim for a middle ground, where the semicolon is used only for the specific purposes described in this chapter.

Linguistic Note

Whether you should use a semicolon, a period, or a comma (plus a coordinating conjunction) to separate independent clauses depends mainly on how strong you want the connection to be. A good discussion of this issue can be found in J. Dawkins, "Teaching Punctuation as a Rhetorical Tool," *College Composition and Communication* 46.4 (December 1995).

Computer Activities

The examples in this chapter will assist students in locating places where they have created a type of comma splice (Chapter 11.3), as in, "More than 185 countries belong to the United Nations, however, only five of them have veto power." It is possible, however, for a conjunctive adverb to be positioned at the beginning of a sentence, as in, "More than 185 countries belong to the United Nations. However, only five of them have veto power." Students can search for the two-sentence cases by capitalizing the conjunctive adverb. It may be that some students routinely avoid putting conjunctive adverbs anywhere but at the beginning of a sentence.

Connections

This section is related to 13.4, on using commas between items in a series.

Connections

This advice is repeated in Part 4, on following standard practice in using other punctuation with quotations.

13.6 **The colon**

Chapter Highlights

The colon is one of the most versatile punctuation marks in English. It serves to introduce a list, appositive, or quotation; it can be used to separate independent clauses; and it is used in titles, letter and memo headings, and numbers and addresses.

Teaching Suggestions

Perhaps the most common mistake students make in using the colon is not placing a grammatically complete clause before it. You may want to spend some class time on this (and refer students to Chapter 11.2, Sentence Fragments).

Linguistic Note

The term *colon* derives from a Greek word meaning "member," "limb," or "clause." It was used in English as early as 1674 to denote a mark used for "marking off a limb or clause of a sentence" (Skeat's *Etymological Dictionary of the English Language*, 1879). It is not related to the identical word that means "large intestine."

13.7 **The apostrophe**

Chapter Highlights

This section of the chapter describes the main uses of the apostrophe: to indicate possession, to indicate contractions and omissions, and to form certain plurals.

Teaching Suggestions

Perhaps because it does not get much attention, the apostrophe is one of the most misused punctuation marks. You may want to give special attention to two types of errors that are particularly common: omission of the apostrophe in singular possessive nouns and insertion of the apostrophe in the possessive pronoun *its*.

Computer Activities

Have students identify possible apostrophe problems in their own writing, as described in the common errors chart in this section of the chapter. Or, if they only have trouble using it's/its, have them restrict their search to just that problem. In either case, they should keep track of whatever errors they find.

Linguistic Note

Nouns in Old English were marked for one of three cases: nominative, accusative, or possessive (genitive). In Middle English, only the possessive was marked, with *es: the Emperoures doghter.* In Modern English, this possessive case marking has been reduced further to 's: *the Emperor's daughter.*

13.8 **Quotation marks**

Chapter Highlights

Although use of quotation marks is not typically a major problem for student writers, it can pose occasional difficulties. This section of the chapter covers the main uses of quotation marks: direct quotations, skepticism, shifts of register, and titles of short works. It also describes at some length how to use quotation marks with other punctuation.

Class Activities

Handmade signs sometimes misuse quotation marks as markers of emphasis, as in "ROOM FOR RENT." Have students look for such signs, either in the community or on personal websites. These examples may be posted by students online in a discussion forum.

Teaching Suggestions

Academic writing conventions are especially scrupulous about the use of sources. It is important for students to clearly understand the difference between quoting the exact words of a source and simply paraphrasing the ideas of a source. It would be a good idea to teach this section along with Chapter 19, on using sources responsibly.

Teaching Suggestions

Quotation marks are often used in editorial columns and letters to the editor, either to indicate a direct quotation or to show skepticism. Have students look in a newspaper for cases illustrating both types of use.

Teaching Suggestions

Students are sometimes tempted to abuse this use of quotation marks. Instead of adhering to an appropriate academic register, they will dot their prose with colloquialisms in quotation marks. Be on guard for this habit.

Connections

This guideline applies mainly to titles of brief works cited in the body of a text. Citations included in a list of references or bibliography may or may not use quotation marks, depending on the documentation system used. Refer students to Chapters 21 through 23 to determine the style of the documentation system used in their field.

Answers for Chapter 13 *You Try It* Exercises

➲ *You Try It* 13.1 Correcting Punctuation Errors

Guess what?

I just found the website for NOFX, which I have been meaning to search out. It's *http://www.nofx.anyserver.com.*

I just got their new CD. It was a real deal at W. E. Jones Music downtown—$12.99. I'm listening to it now. It rules.

That's it for now. I have to write a paper (yuck) due Tuesday. It's on FDR and WWII. Got to go.

Later. :-)

➲ *You Try It* 13.2 Adding End Punctuation

1. How long have human beings been concerned about population growth? If you believe the warnings, we have long been on the verge of overpopulating the earth. In a warning written around AD

200, a Roman writer named Tertullian lamented that "we are burdensome to the world and the resources are scarcely adequate to us." The population at the time is believed to have been 200 million, barely 3 percent of today's 5.8 billion. He thought he had reason for concern!

2. Can a program ever be believed once it stages an incident? Sometimes it can. NBC's *Dateline* was not the first network to fake a car crash when it used igniters in its dramatization of the hazards of GM trucks; all three networks had done the same. Unfortunately, the public was not told that program personnel "helped" ignite the fire. Why did the network do it? They did it because of competition for viewers. The line between entertainment and news was badly blurred. What was the reason for the media error? *Dateline* anchor Jane Pauley replied, "Because on one side of the line is an Emmy; the other, the abyss."

➲ *You Try It* 13.3 Correcting Comma Errors

1. In comparison with ordinary soap, the production of detergents exerts a more intense environmental impact.
2. Three out of four Americans claim to believe in God, and four out of ten go to church regularly.
3. If a typical book contains 500 pages, the information content of a single chromosome corresponds to some 4,000 volumes.
4. There are numerous private daycare centers in the U.S., but the employees are often underpaid and weary from looking after too many children.
5. In many countries, people cannot conceive of themselves apart from the family or group they belong to. In America, on the other hand, self-reliance is the fundamental virtue.
6. The English language surrounds us like a sea, and, like the waters of the deep, it is full of mysteries.
7. Of all the world's languages (which now number some 2,700), English is arguably the richest in vocabulary.
8. For most people, body temperature drops at night and then rises in the morning.
9. Enjoyment and appreciation are related terms, but they are not synonymous.

10. Although one can enjoy music without understanding it, appreciation of music requires some knowledge.

➲ *You Try It* 13.4 Correcting Comma Errors

1. The anti-tax group collected 65,202 signatures on a petition in support of an immediate tax cut.
2. Although this is more than the required 64,928 signatures, it still may not be enough.
3. Because of duplications, illegible signatures, and people improperly signing for other family members, a minimum margin of at least 2,000 is usually needed to withstand challenges, experts say.
4. At one time, many states often barred the sale of contraceptives to minors, prohibited the display of contraceptives, or even banned their sale altogether.
5. Today condoms are sold in the grocery store, and some television stations even air ads for them.
6. The capital campaign, which was off to a great start, hoped to net $1.2 million.
7. When we shop, we want to get the most for our money.
8. Herbalists practice herbal medicine, which is based on the medicinal qualities of plants or herbs.
9. Economically and culturally overshadowed by the United States, Canada has nonetheless managed to carve out a feisty, independent identity since World War II.
10. The participants, who had been carefully chosen by Akron's political and community establishment, expressed a range of views.

➲ *You Try It* 13.5 Correcting Comma Errors

1. One fictitious address used by advertisers is John and Mary Jones, 100 Main Street, Anytown, USA 12345.
2. We are a nation of shoppers, aren't we?
3. Easy access to birth control, however, was not always the case.
4. "It would be good to have this question on the ballot," the governor said.
5. This sentence is correct as it is.
6. For example, he would sometimes say, "Let justice roll down like the waters."
7. A Renoir exhibition, organized and first shown by the National Gallery of Canada in Ottawa, Ontario, opened at the Art Institute of

Chicago on October 21, 1997, and ran through January 4th of the next year.

8. Much to the irritation of its neighbor, for instance, Canada keeps friendly ties with Fidel Castro's Cuba.
9. Lee surrendered to Grant at Appomattox Court House, Virginia, on April 9, 1865.
10. According to the police, there were more than 10,000 protestors at the rally.

➲ *You Try It* 13.6 Removing Unnecessary Commas

1. Tiger Woods has more competition than he did five years ago.
2. My favorite sports are team sports such as basketball and football.
3. Anyone who appreciates classic art would enjoy a visit to the Prado Museum in Madrid.
4. The cues of daylight and darkness help to keep plants and animals synchronized with the environment.
5. This sentence is correct as is.
6. Although they often find Americans welcoming and friendly, this is not altogether an easy country for foreigners to travel in.
7. Rodney gave his girlfriend a necklace with a beautiful large black gemstone in it.
8. I normally use the Internet portal *Yahoo!*, but my mother prefers *Excite*.
9. The objective of the American school system is to bestow a broad education on every youngster.
10. Unless they frequently trade in their car for a new one, people normally search for a car that will last many years.

➲ *You Try It* 13.7 Correcting Punctuation Errors

1. Socrates disliked being called a "teacher"; he preferred to think of himself as an intellectual midwife.
2. Tests will be given on the following dates: Monday, November 2; Friday, November 20; and Monday, December 7.
3. The scientific naming and classification of all organisms is known as *taxonomy*; both living and extinct organisms are taxonomically classified.
4. A single category of a species is called a *taxon*; multiple categories are *taxa*.

5. Since laughter seems to help the body heal, many doctors and hospitals are prescribing humor for their patients.
6. Beethoven was deaf when he wrote his final symphonies; nevertheless, they are considered musical masterpieces.
7. Some people think that watching a video at home is more fun than going to a movie; movie theaters are often crowded and noisy.
8. The lifeguards closed the beach when a shark was spotted; a few hours later, some fishermen reported seeing the shark leave, so the beach was reopened.
9. The feeling of balance is controlled by the ears; inside each ear are three small tubes filled with fluid.
10. Since its opening in 1955, Disneyland has been an important part of American culture; it has the ability to reflect and reinforce American beliefs, values, and ideals.

⮭ *You Try It* 13.8 Correcting Apostrophe Errors

1. It's unfortunate that Bob's birthday falls on February 29.
2. I wanted to go to Maria and Roberto's party, but I wasn't able to.
3. The snake sheds its skin many times during its life.
4. Does the men's group meet here?
5. No, it's a women's group that meets in this room on Thursdays.
6. I can't wait 'til my vacation comes!
7. I'm taking my lawyer's advice on such matters.
8. All of the orchestra members' instruments seemed to be out of tune.
9. The driver's and passenger's airbags both deployed after the accident.
10. Kevin and Lauren's older sister is in high school now.

Chapter 14 / *Spelling and Mechanics*

MULTIMEDIA FOR CHAPTER 14

VIDEO TUTORIALS	SAMPLE DOCUMENTS	WRITING ACTIVITIES
Video 14.1 Chapter Introduction	Chart Homophones	*You Try It* 14.1 Personal Spelling Demons
Video 14.2 Speeding Up Spell Checking		*You Try It* 14.2 Correcting Spelling Errors in Sentences
Video 14.3 Spelling Errors		*You Try It* 14.3 Correcting Spelling Errors in a Paragraph
Video 14.4 Slang Spellings		*You Try It* 14.4 Combining Words and Suffixes
Video 14.5 Capitalization Errors		*You Try It* 14.5 Combining a Root Word and Suffix
		You Try It 14.6 Making Words Plural
		You Try It 14.7 Inserting the Correct Form of *ei*

		You Try It 14.8 Correcting Capitalization Errors
		You Try It 14.9 Adding Italics

14.1 Spelling

Chapter Highlights

Spelling is a problem for most student writers, even in this age of spell-checkers. Spell-checkers are imperfect tools that must be backed up with good, old-fashioned human scrutiny. This chapter encourages students to use a spell-checker appropriately, master the most troublesome homonyms, guard against the most common spelling errors, and learn basic spelling rules and patterns. The chapter contains a list of commonly misused homophones and a list of commonly misspelled words—both of which will be useful later for reference purposes. It also contains a Help box on how to speed up spell-checking.

Learning Outcomes

The learning outcomes for Chapter 14 are listed in the chart below, along with the relevant sections of the chapter and exercises that teachers can use to evaluate their students' mastery of the objectives. This chart also appears as a clickable link in the etext.

CHAPTER 14 LEARNING OUTCOMES CHART	
To assess your understanding of the Chapter 14 learning outcomes, work the corresponding You Try It exercises and study the relevant chapter sections.	
14.1 Improve your spelling.	*You Try It* 14.1 Personal Spelling Demons

	You Try It 14.2 Correcting Spelling Errors in Sentences
	You Try It 14.3 Correcting Spelling Errors in a Paragraph
	You Try It 14.4 Combining Words and Suffixes
	You Try It 14.5 Combining a Root Word and Suffix
	You Try It 14.6 Making Words Plural
	You Try It 14.7 Inserting the Correct Form of *ei*
14.2 Understand and use conventions for capital letters.	*You Try It* 14.8 Correcting Capitalization Errors
14.3 Understand and use conventions for italics.	*You Try It* 14.9 Adding Italics

Teaching Suggestions

Spend some class time talking about the importance of good spelling. In all academic classes and in life outside of academia, poor spelling is noticed and can reflect badly on the writer. Research shows, for example, that poor spelling in a résumé or job letter can negate good credentials and eliminate the applicant from consideration.

Computer Activities

Encourage students to explore the different features and options on the spell checker. Make sure that they do the two activities described in the video.

Class Activities

Ask students which of the homophones on the list they find most troublesome. Make a note of these words, and later include them in some exercise sentences similar to those in *You Try It* 14.2. Also, ask students if there are any homophones they have trouble with that are not included in the list.

Class Activities

1. Ask students which of the words on the list of commonly misspelled words they have the most trouble with. Also ask them whether there are other words not on the list that should be. Make note of students' answers and prepare some exercise sentences that include the words.

2. Have students write a coherent paragraph using at least eight commonly misspelled words. These paragraphs may be posted online in a discussion forum.

14.2 Capital letters

Chapter Highlights

This section of the chapter covers problems that students have with capitalization: whether to capitalize the first word of a sentence, whether to capitalize names and titles, which words to capitalize in a title, and whether to capitalize email addresses and URLs.

Additional Exercises

Give students a text in which you have changed all the uppercase letters to lowercase ones. (Use the CHANGE CASE command on your word processor.) Challenge them to restore the text to its original form.

Class Activities

While some contemporary poets capitalize the first letter of each line, others do not. Find an example of each type of capitalization and have students discuss the effects of the two styles. This activity may be done online in a discussion forum or chat room.

Connections

Following this rule requires students to know exactly what a sentence is. You may want to refer some of your students to Chapter 11.

Class Activities

1. Intercaps—capital letters used in the middle of a word (for example, *PowerMac* or *PageMaker*)—are common in the computer industry. Have students come up with ten or more names with intercaps, and then ask them why they think the creators of these names chose to style them as they did. This exercise is fun, and it requires students to consider some of the functionality behind capitalization.

2. Students often do not know whether to capitalize the names of academic courses and disciplines. In their confusion, they may capitalize *physics* everywhere it occurs, or they may never capitalize it at all. Or they may randomly capitalize it in some places and not in others. Have them look through the college catalog and construct their own theory about the capitalization of academic course names and discipline names. Have them cite examples to back up their theories. Lead a class discussion on this topic. This activity may be conducted online in a discussion forum or chat room.

14.3 Italics

Chapter Highlights

This section of the chapter covers elements that require italics or underlining: titles of independent creative works; Internet addresses; names of particular vehicles; foreign expressions; words, letters, and numbers referred to as such; and emphasized words and phrases.

Class Activities

Sometimes (particularly in textbooks), bold font is used for emphasis instead of underlining or italicization. Have students examine their textbooks from other courses to see which format is used. Compile the results into a summary chart, and discuss. This activity may be done online in a discussion forum.

Answers for Chapter 14 *You Try It* Exercises

➲ *You Try It* 14.1 Personal Spelling Demons

Answers will vary.

➲ *You Try It* 14.2 Correcting Spelling Errors in Sentences

1. The doctor *whose* license was revoked by the medical *board* is no longer allowed to treat *patients*.
2. The television *diary* is one of the devices used by A. C. Nielsen to research the programs people choose.
3. The *piece* of *advice* Ann Landers gave was simple, practical, and *fair*.
4. The poster *cited* Jesse Jackson, who said, "Your children need your *presence* more than your *presents*."
5. Because he is an excellent magician, he always allows the audience a *thorough* inspection of his props before he creates his wonderful *illusions*.
6. More than once last *week*, the tardy student managed to *elude* the *principal* as she entered the building.
7. At a gorgeous *site* atop a hill, the women gathered for a bonding *rite*, calling forth the *immanent* wisdom from each person present.
8. The *personnel* department's intense search for a *principal* engineer to *lead* the department led to the promotion of a woman whose talent had *formerly* gone unrecognized.
9. When the camouflaged *guerrilla heard* something moving in the underbrush, he tried to determine *whether* it was an enemy soldier.
10. The small craft carrying *illicit* drugs encountered bad *weather* that night and traveled far from *its* intended *course*.

➲ *You Try It* 14.3 Correcting Spelling Errors in a Paragraph

On the second *Wednesday* in *February*, those running for various positions in town *government* gathered for a *Candidates'* Night. At the event, the two *candidates* for school *committee* expressed *different* opinions about how to *accommodate* the new state education standards without having to *exceed* the available amount of money. Mr. Smith believes that the state legislature is right to make *foreign* language a required course. He also pointed out that an up-to-date school *library* is *necessary* for student *success.* Ms. Jones, on the other hand, *basically* believes that, although *beneficial,* both *foreign* language courses and school *libraries* are less important than other things, such as regular school building *maintenance.* The *candidates* then had an *argument* about building *maintenance,* Ms. Jones *recommending* that the town *seize* the opportunity to repair current buildings and Mr. Smith stating that the *maintenance* budget is *exaggerated* and proposing that the town defer some of the repairs in order to spend more on educational programming. Because the debate highlighted *noticeable differences* between the *candidates,* the voters who attended the event were well served.

➲ *You Try It* 14.4 Combining Words and Suffixes

1. completely
2. gracious
3. grievance
4. wholesomeness
5. exercising
6. traceable
7. continuous
8. solely
9. argument
10. sedative

➲ *You Try It* 14.5 Combining a Root Word and Suffix

1. roommate
2. hesitantly
3. shopping
4. controllable
5. plausible
6. cooler
7. drastically
8. quietest
9. thinness
10. publicly

➲ *You Try It* 14.6 Making Words Plural

1. devices
2. memorandums, memoranda
3. churches

4. geese
5. moose
6. kisses
7. skies
8. syllabuses, syllabi
9. mailboxes
10. mice (for little furry creatures); mouses (for computer devices)

⊃ *You Try It* 14.7 Inserting the Correct Form of ei

1. experience
2. perceive
3. height
4. chief
5. vein
6. deceit
7. foreign
8. thief
9. beige
10. ancient

⊃ *You Try It* 14.8 Correcting Capitalization Errors

1. On July 17, 1996, a Trans World Airlines passenger plane crashed into the Atlantic Ocean, killing all 230 people aboard.
2. Bound for Paris, France, the Boeing 747 disappeared from radar screens at 8:48 P.M.
3. The plane was about fifty miles east of the airport when it plunged into the ocean about ten miles south of East Moriches, Long Island.
4. The U.S. Coast Guard conducted a futile rescue effort, and the National Transportation Safety Board carried out a long investigation.
5. Meanwhile, rumors circulated on the Internet and a well-known politician claimed, "The plane was shot down by a U.S. Navy missile."
6. I logged on to *http://www.cbpp.org/pa-1.htm* and found a report called "Pulling Apart: A State-by-State Analysis of Income Trends."
7. The report, published by the Center on Budget and Policy Priorities, says that "in 48 states, the gap between the incomes of the richest 20 percent of families with children and the incomes of the poorest 20 percent of families with children is significantly

wider than it was two decades ago." (Only Alaska and North Dakota bucked the trend.)

8.   Individual states could counteract this national trend (few, however, have done so).

9.   My nephew, Julius Evans, Jr., is a junior at San Francisco State University.

10. So, we'll sit no more a'writing
     So late into the night,
     Though our minds be still a burning,
     And our thoughts be still as bright.

⊃ *You Try It* 14.9 Adding Italics

1.   My favorite poem in Robert Creeley's book *For Love* is "A Wicker Basket."

2.   Juan says the new drama teacher is very *simpático.*

3.   Of the fifty people interviewed, twenty-two said that 13 is an unlucky number.

4.   You can keep track of the spaceship *NEAR*'s progress at *http://spacelink.nasa.gov/.*

5.   Smoking also contributes to *platelet adhesiveness,* or the sticking together of red blood cells that is associated with blood clots.

6.   She's an easy teacher—she gives all A's and B's. [No change from original, although it would not be incorrect to italicize A and B.]

7.   For me, the best track on Fleetwood Mac's *Greatest Hits* is "Rhiannon."

8.   The flower that does best under these conditions is the prairie zinnia (*Zinnia grandiflora*).

9.   For further information, email us at *johnsonco@waterworks.com.*

10. The term *dementia* implies deficits in memory, spatial orientation, language, or personality. This definition sets it apart from delirium, which usually involves changing levels of consciousness, restlessness, confusion, and hallucinations.

Chapter 15 / *For Multilingual Writers*

MULTIMEDIA FOR CHAPTER 15

VIDEO TUTORIALS	SAMPLE DOCUMENTS	WRITING ACTIVITIES
Video 15.1 Chapter Introduction	Chart Common Examples of Two-Way Nouns	*You Try It* 15.1 Selecting Count and Noncount Nouns
	Chart Modal Auxiliaries Ranked by Strength	*You Try It* 15.2 Using *the* Appropriately
		You Try It 15.3 Inserting *a, an,* or *the* into Sentences
		You Try It 15.4 Inserting *a, an,* or *the* into Paragraphs
		You Try It 15.5 Using Correct Verb Forms
		You Try It 15.6 Correcting Verb Forms
		You Try It 15.7 Choosing Correct Verb Forms

Chapter Highlights

This chapter addresses two major aspects of English grammar that often are troublesome for nonnative speakers--especially those whose native languages do not work the same say. First, the chapter provides tips on nouns and articles. Then the chapter provides tips on verbs.

Learning Outcomes

The learning outcomes for Chapter 15 are listed in the following chart, along with the relevant sections of the chapter and exercises that teachers can use to evaluate their students' mastery of the objectives. This chart also appears as a clickable link in the etext.

CHAPTER 15 LEARNING OUTCOMES CHART	
To assess your understanding of the Chapter 15 learning outcomes, work the corresponding You Try It exercises and study the relevant chapter sections.	
15.1 Understand the unique features and forms of written English.	*You Try It* 15.1 Selecting Count and Noncount Nouns
15.2 Recognize and correct some common problems with English nouns and articles.	*You Try It* 15.2 Using *the* Appropriately *You Try It* 15.3 Inserting *a, an,* or *the* into Sentences *You Try It* 15.4 Inserting *a, an,* or *the* into Paragraphs

15.3 Recognize and correct some common problems with English verbs.	*You Try It* 15.5 Using Correct Verb Forms
	You Try It 15.6 Correcting Verb Forms
	You Try It 15.7 Choosing Correct Verb Forms

15.1 Tips on nouns and articles

Teaching Suggestions

Many nonnative speakers subconsciously downplay the importance of articles, thinking that if their native language does not use them, they must not be all that important. Furthermore, articles do not have content in the way that nouns, verbs, adjectives, and adverbs do. Speakers reason that they can convey their basic meaning without using articles. Although this is true, articles play a significant role in the English language. By distinguishing between definiteness and indefiniteness and between countability and noncountability, articles make communication much more precise than it otherwise would be. As a teacher, you have probably experienced the confusion that arises when a nonnative speaker misuses articles. Use this experience to convince students that learning to use articles correctly is well worth the effort. Tell them that articles are not just window dressing, but that they help guide readers through a text. Misusing articles means more work for the reader, as well as unnecessary confusion and irritation.

Linguistic Note

One can refer to an entire class of things with either the definite article (*the earthworm*), the indefinite article (*an earthworm*), or the simple plural (*earthworms*). There are subtle differences in meaning among these three, but the differences are so slight that they are usually not worth taking up class time to discuss.

Class Activities

Fill-in-the blank exercises like *You Try It* 15.2 are easy to create. If you have a little extra time, we suggest you create an exercise of your own, tailored to the interests of the class. For example, you might extract a paragraph or two from one of the class readings or from a recent campus news story and retype it, leaving blank spaces in place of every *a, an,* or *the* and in front of every noun that does not have a determiner like *these, our, some,* and *no.* This activity may be done online in a discussion forum.

Linguistic Note

College students are often curious about why people say *the University of Michigan* but not *Michigan State University.* It has to do not with the sizes of the two institutions but with the simple linguistic fact that the former has a modifier (*of Michigan*) following the head noun *University,* while the latter does not. The same principle explains why people say *the College of William and Mary* but *Lewis and Clark College.*

15.1 **Tips on verbs**

Chapter Highlights

Not all verbs are covered in this section of the chapter--only those dealing with phrasal verbs, verb complements, verbs of state, modal auxiliary verbs, and conditional sentences. Thus, the focus is on verbs as vocabulary items, not on tense, voice, mood, or other aspects of verb grammar.

Teaching Suggestions

1. The material in this section of the chapter cannot be mastered in a short period of time. Therefore, your goal in teaching the chapter should be simply to focus students' attention on the general patterns, so that they can proceed to learn the detailed material on their own. One general pattern, for example, is that verbs of state cannot occur in the progressive tense. Over time, students will gradually master the correct use of verbs of state.

2. Students should be encouraged to keep a personal dictionary of phrasal verbs. However, as there are thousands of phrasal verbs in the English language, urge students to look for other sources as well as the dictionary and to let their dictionaries grow slowly over time, in the

manner of a personal journal or diary. Phrasal verbs are common in everyday speech; indeed, they are a prime feature of colloquial English. Thus, they are worth whatever class time you can spend on them.

Class Activities

Have each student find a new phrasal verb outside of class, learn as much about it as possible (starting with a dictionary definition), and then present it in class as a challenge to the other students. The other students try to guess its meaning and its syntactic features--that is, whether it is transitive or intransitive, separable or inseparable--and try to use it in a sentence.

Answers for Chapter 15 *You Try It* Exercises

➲ *You Try It* 15.1 Selecting Count and Noncount Nouns

1. idea, *ideas*
2. money; countable or noncountable; sometimes pluralized when referring to government financial assets--for example, *state tax monies*
3. math problem, *math problems*
4. government; countable or noncountable; can be pluralized when used in the countable sense to refer to particular governments
5. party, *parties*
6. memorization, noncountable
7. computer program, *computer programs*
8. silence; almost always noncountable
9. tobacco; countable or noncountable; can be pluralized to refer to different types of tobacco
10. movie, *movies*

➲ *You Try It* 15.2 Using *the* Appropriately

Do animals have morals? Many people do not think so. Those who would put _____ humans on a pedestal above all other creatures feel threatened by __*the*__ possibility of morality in _____ animals, since it seems to threaten __*the*__ special and unique status of _____ humans. This idea that _____ humans are __*the*__ most virtuous creatures usually comes from _____ religion, so to say _____ animals can be moral is sometimes perceived as a threat against some deeply held religious beliefs. But it's

149

not. The only thing that is threatened by __*the*__ proposition that _____ animals are _____ moral beings is __*the*__ belief that _____ morality alone defines our "human nature." [M. Bekoff, *The Emotional Lives of Animals*, p. 90]

⮑ *You Try It* 15.3 Inserting *a, an,* or *the* into Sentences

1. Sarah used to play _____ soccer for her high school team, and she was __*the*__ star player.
2. He gave me _____ good advice.
3. __*An*__ anecdote is __*a*__ type of illustration.
4. You should give credit to __*the*__ people who did __*the*__ work.
5. __*The*__ professor surprised __*the*__ students with __*a*__ quiz.
6. All of __*the*__ dogs in __*the*__ neighborhood started to bark when __*the*__ power went out.
7. Vera bought __*a*__ new pink dress for graduation, but, unfortunately, __*the*__ dress was too big.

⮑ *You Try It* 15.4 Inserting *a, an,* or *the* into Paragraphs

1. In _____ different societies, _____ gift giving is usually ritualized. __*A*__ ritual is __*a*__ set of multiple, symbolic behaviors that occurs in __*a*__ fixed sequence. Gift-giving rituals in our society usually involve the choosing of __*a*__ proper gift by __*the*__ giver, __*the*__ removing of __*the*__ price tag, wrapping of __*the*__ gift, timing __*the*__ gift giving, and waiting for __*the*__ reaction (either positive or negative) from __*the*__ recipient.

2. In __*the*__ latter part of __*the*__ nineteenth century, _____ capitalism was characterized by __*the*__ growth of _____ giant corporations. Control of most of __*the*__ important industries became more and more concentrated. Accompanying this concentration of industry was __*an*__ equally striking concentration of _____ income in __*the*__ hands of a small percentage of __*the*__ population.

⮑ *You Try It* 15.5 Using Correct Verb Forms

1. Professor Adams refused (change) __*to change*__ the student's grade.
2. The student believed that (change) __*changing*__ the grade was the only fair course of action.

3. The student also insisted on (discuss) *discussing* the matter with the dean of the college.
4. The student hoped (convince) *to convince* the dean that the professor was being unjust in her refusal to change the grade.
5. The dean, however, decided (side) *to side* with the professor, so the student's grade was never changed from a B to an A.
6. The famous scientist offered (speak) *to speak* at the university graduation ceremony.
7. Most students dislike (study) *studying* for final examinations.

➲ *You Try It* 15.6 Correcting Verb Forms

The correct verb form is italicized below.

1. A formal academic essay usually *contains* an introduction, the main discussion, and a conclusion.
2. My parents *will* send me some money.
3. A thesis statement should *present* the main idea of the essay.
4. Right now, Marinela *is studying* in the library for a test in her one o'clock class.
5. Yuka could not *imagine missing* even a day of her ESL conversation class.
6. Many students enjoy *studying* in small groups.
7. Many students *do not understand* that the organization of an essay is as important as its content.

➲ *You Try It* 15.7 Choosing Correct Verb Forms

The correct verb form is italicized below.

1. If Frank studied harder, he (got, *would get,* will get) better grades.
2. Whenever Suzy turns on her computer, she (*gets*, would get, will get) an error message.
3. If we plan ahead, we (finish, *should finish*, would finish) the project on schedule.
4. You will disappoint your parents unless you (*call*, may call, should call) them soon.
5. If the rain (stopped, has stopped, *had stopped*) sooner, there would not have been so much flooding.
6. If Serena Williams retires, tennis (loses, should lose, *will lose*) one of its most exciting players.

7. Just when you think things can't get worse, they sometimes (*do*, might, would).

8. Unless the price of oil comes down, world financial markets (are, *will be*, would be) in trouble.

9. If you like good art, you (go, will go, *should go*) to the Guggenheim Museum in New York.

10. If Mozart had lived a full life, he (composed, had composed, *might have composed*) much more music.

PART**FOUR**

Research

CHAPTER 16 / *The Research Project*

MULTIMEDIA FOR CHAPTER 16

VIDEO TUTORIALS	SAMPLE DOCUMENTS	WRITING ACTIVITIES
Video 16.1 Chapter Introduction	Chart A Strategy for Writing a Research Paper	*You Try It* 16.1 Understanding the Research Assignment
Video 16.2 Choosing a Research Topic	Chart Understanding Cue Words in Assignments	*You Try It* 16.2 Investigating Topics
Video 16.23 Using Google and Google Scholar Effectively	Chart Schedules for Writing a Research Paper	*You Try It* 16.3 Making a Schedule
Video 16.4 Using a Computer Bibliography Program	Example Document Comment	*You Try It* 16.4 Working on a Bibliography
	Example Annotated Internet Printout	*You Try It* 16.5 Investigating Background Sources

	Example Annotated Bibliography	*You Try It* 16.6 Primary Research
	Example Library Catalog Entry	
	Example Electronic Resources	
	Guidelines Conducting Effective Observations	
	Guidelines Conducting Effective Interviews	

Chapter Highlights

This chapter introduces students to the research process and encourages them to think of themselves as researchers. Students are taught to think in terms of seeking the answer to a question or confirming a hypothesis, rather than simply locating enough sources to write a term paper. This chapter leads students through the process of finding a pertinent topic, narrowing it by posing research questions and developing a hypothesis, outlining a search strategy, and making a schedule. Students are encouraged to begin a research notebook and a working bibliography. One unique feature of this chapter is its emphasis on gathering background information before conducting focused research. I have found that students need to begin with background searching; only in this way are they able to ask the right questions and formulate a hypothesis that can be investigated during more focused research.

Learning Outcomes

The learning outcomes for Chapter 16 are listed in the following chart, along with the relevant sections of the chapter and exercises that teachers can use to evaluate their students' mastery of the objectives. This chart also appears as a clickable link in the etext.

CHAPTER 16 LEARNING OUTCOMES CHART	
To assess your understanding of the Chapter 16 learning outcomes, work the corresponding You Try It exercises and study the relevant chapter sections.	
16.1 Understand what it means to do research.	*You Try It* 16.1 Understanding the Research Assignment *You Try It* 16.2 Investigating Topics
16.2 Create a search strategy and schedule.	*You Try It* 16.3 Making a Schedule *You Try It* 16.4 Working on a Bibliography
16.3 Conduct focused research.	*You Try It* 16.5 Investigating Background Sources *You Try It* 16.6 Primary Research

16.1 Become a researcher

Teaching Suggestions

This section stresses the importance of research and the ways in which researchers go about accomplishing their task. When first assigned a research paper, students are often overwhelmed by the magnitude of the project. But when they break down their topic into its component parts, it becomes much more manageable. As you teach this section, encourage students to begin by trying to understand what the research assignment is asking them to do. Then they should select and focus on a topic so that it is workable, given the constraints of the assignment; ask research questions; develop a hypothesis; and outline a search strategy. These steps will help students to systematically map out their own research agendas.

Class Activities

1. Discuss with students the parameters of the research assignment (either in person or online in a discussion forum). Stress that they are to conduct research in order to investigate a question or solve a problem that intrigues them. Help them understand that they already know how to be researchers, since they have all researched some problem or question: which car to buy, which courses to take, whom to date, what cereal or computer or shampoo to purchase. The research they are about to embark on is not qualitatively different from the research they have already done. It simply differs in scope. Brainstorm possible topics as a class and write them on the blackboard or whiteboard.

2. Bring to class or post online a short example of a report that describes a primary research project, and compare it with another report that uses only secondary research. Students need to understand and appreciate the difference between primary and secondary research.

3. Bring to class or post online several news magazines and a few scholarly journals. Have students browse through them to see what kinds of research are represented. Discuss their findings.

4. Ask students to bring to class or post online any research assignments that they have been given in other classes they are taking. Compile a list on an overhead transparency or on the blackboard or whiteboard for class discussion. Talk about the purpose, audience, and types of research required by the assignments.

Collaborative Activities

Ask students to outline their search strategies. Make sure the outlines specifically identify particular indexes, Internet sources (e.g., *Google Scholar*), databases, and so on to be used in the search. Have students share and discuss their search strategies in groups of three or four.

Computer Activities

1. Demonstrate an Internet search as a method of finding a topic. Use a search engine with subject directories to help students see how they might narrow their topics productively.

2. Discuss key word searching on the Internet. (Refer to Chapter 17 for more information.)

16.2 **Make a schedule**

Teaching Suggestions

Students often vastly underestimate the amount of time needed to complete a major research paper. This chapter tries to help students learn how to allocate their time appropriately. You might talk about a research project you have done or initiate a discussion among students about writing projects they have completed in the past. In particular, it is important to encourage them to start early and to work systematically.

Class Activities

Project overhead the sample schedule guidelines chart in this section. Discuss with your class the number of days or weeks you anticipate each step will take. Have them make a calendar on which they commit to a completion date for tasks in each week during the process. Check their research notebooks on each due date to ensure that they are keeping on top of the project. This activity may also be done in a computer classroom using an LCD projector.

Computer Activities

If your word-processing or e-mail system has a CALENDAR feature, suggest that students make use of it in their planning.

16.2a **Create a research notebook**

Teaching Suggestions

Build process points into your grading scheme by having students turn in their research notebooks periodically for completion points. Grading their processes merely involves determining whether or not they did the work, so it should not take much of your time. However, it is extremely worthwhile, because when you review their research notebooks, you learn which students are falling behind and where they are having trouble. Furthermore, you avoid getting any plagiarized research papers turned in at the eleventh hour—you can simply refuse to accept any papers for which you have not seen and graded all the process work in the research notebook.

Class Activities

Model effective note taking for students. Help students set up an effective note taking system that they can adhere to, whether it involves a paper or electronic notebook.

Computer Activities

1. Show students how to organize a folder that contains separate files for different aspects of the research project: a folder for the research notebook, another for the bibliography, a third for the first draft, and so on.

2. Ask students to email their electronic research notebooks to you periodically for your review and grading of their research processes. Have students email the notebooks as a file attachment that you can download and read on your office computer. Use the DOCUMENT COMMENTS feature to provide students with feedback, and then email the notebooks back to the individual students.

3. Demonstrate how the DOCUMENT COMMENTS feature can be used as a note taking device.

4. Use a note taking/bibliography software program to keep track of research notes and sources.

16.2b Create a working bibliography

Teaching Suggestions

Students often run into trouble when they do not accurately note where source information was found. Help them begin a working bibliography and discuss the kinds of information they should be keeping track of. In particular, students who are using Internet sources often forget to note the exact URL of the source and the date of its posting or copyright. Encourage students to keep accurate and complete information so that they avoid having to track down sources later.

Class Activities

1. Project a copy of Kaycee's working bibliography. Discuss with the class the types of sources and the kinds of information students need to

record in their own working bibliographies. Remind them that they may not necessarily cite in the final bibliography every source listed in the working bibliography, because not every source consulted will actually be used in the final paper.

2. Project an annotated bibliography. Discuss with students how to write this type of bibliography. Then ask them to write an annotation (a one- or two-sentence description) for every item in their working bibliography.

3. These two activities may also be done in an online classroom using the file-sharing space and discussion forum.

Computer Activities

1. Demonstrate for students any computer bibliography programs that are available to them such as *NoodleBib!* Caution them that such programs, while helpful, do not eliminate the need for careful proofreading by the writer.

2. Demonstrate for students how to download and print sources they find on the Internet. Remind them to get complete bibliographic information for each source.

16.3 **Gather additional background information**

Teaching Suggestions

One unique feature of this chapter is the suggestion that students begin their research by assessing their own knowledge, rather than dashing off to the library. If students think through their own potential engagement with the topic, then they will have a more successful experience. Next, before they begin to search in a more focused way, I recommend that students get a better grasp of their topic through background reading—consulting with reference librarians, browsing through reference works and bibliographies, and entering discussion groups or talking to experts.

Class Activities

1. Bring to class or post online examples of the various background and reference tools described in this chapter. Alternatively, bring students to the library for a hands-on demonstration. You will no doubt find

that several students have never before talked with a reference librarian or opened a specialized encyclopedia, for example. Class time spent exploring these sources is time well spent.

2. Invite a reference librarian to your classroom to discuss various reference tools with students. You can invite a librarian to take part in an online chat with your students if you are teaching online.

Computer Activities

1. Demonstrate key word searching using Boolean operators. Have students conduct a model search in class and discuss the results.

2. Search for reference works on the Internet. Encourage students to visit reference sites like *refdesk.com* to become familiar with what is available through this online medium.

16.4 Conduct focused research

Teaching Suggestions

This section provides students with explicit guidance in using reference tools that will help them find specific information on their topics. They are instructed in the use of the computerized library catalog, library online databases to locate periodicals and journals, and other online sources. Understanding how to use these tools is crucial to successful secondary research.

Computer Activities

1. Demonstrate searching your library's online catalog. Be sure to search for books, magazines, journals, and newspapers. Reinforce the importance of searching by subject and appropriate keywords.

2. Demonstrate searching for top news stories by using an online newspaper database such as *ProQuest Newsstand.*

Connections

For an outline of how to integrate a research paper assignment into a freshman English course, see James Strickland, "The Research Sequence: What to Do before the Term Paper," *CCC* 37 (May 1986): 233–36.

16.5 **Conduct primary or field research**

This section introduces students to primary research and suggests that, where appropriate, they should consider using primary data as a part of their research project.

Class Activities

Brainstorm with students possible primary research that would add an interesting dimension to their projects. Following a secondary research project with a primary research project on the same topic is a useful and interesting experience for students. While you are grading their research papers, you can have them conduct primary research and report their findings to the class. Primary research can be done individually or in groups.

Collaborative Activities

Have students work in pairs interviewing each other, recording their interview data and reporting to the class what they found out about their classmate. Discuss with your class what makes an effective or ineffective interview.

Answers for Chapter 16 *You Try It* Exercises

For all exercises in this chapter, answers will vary.

CHAPTER 17 / *Using the Internet for Research*

MULTIMEDIA FOR CHAPTER 17

VIDEO TUTORIALS	SAMPLE DOCUMENTS	WRITING ACTIVITIES
Video 17.1 Chapter Introduction	Example Firefox Browser	*You Try It* 17.1 Getting to Know the Internet
Video 17.2 Using the Favorites or History Feature	Example Internet Explorer Browser	*You Try It* 17.2 Understanding Copyright
Video 17.3 Kaycee's Library Database Search	Guidelines Using Web Materials Ethically	*You Try It* 17.3 Finding Online Documents
Video 17.4 Kaycee's Internet Search	Example Google Directory for Topic Search	*You Try It* 17.4 Beginning a Search
	Guidelines Using Boolean Operators	
	Guidelines Finding Government Documents	
	Guidelines Finding Online Periodicals	

Chapter Highlights

The dedication of this entire chapter to using the Internet for research is a unique feature of the etext. Although the Internet has become the single most important factor in research projects, this chapter offers a balanced approach, suggesting to students that the information found on the Internet is but one piece of the larger puzzle. The chapter covers the ways in which the Internet can help students at all stages of the research process—from exploring topics to conducting background and focused searching to collaborating and exchanging feedback. This chapter also teaches students how to search library subscription databases productively. It includes guideline boxes that feature search tools, search tips, and useful Internet sites.

Learning Outcomes

The learning outcomes for Chapter 17 are listed in the following chart, along with the relevant sections of the chapter and exercises that teachers can use to evaluate their students' mastery of the objectives. This chart also appears as a clickable link in the etext.

CHAPTER 17 LEARNING OUTCOMES CHART	
To assess your understanding of the Chapter 17 learning outcomes, work the corresponding *You Try It* exercises and study the relevant chapter sections.	
17.1 Understand how to use the Internet to do research.	*You Try It* 17.1 Getting to Know the Internet *You Try It* 17.2 Understanding Copyright
17.2 Understand how to use search tools.	*You Try It* 17.3 Finding Online Documents
17.3 Understand how to search library databases and the Internet.	*You Try It* 17.4 Beginning a Search

17.1 Use Internet sources through the research process

Teaching Suggestions

This section stresses use of the Internet at all stages of the research process. Encourage students to use the Internet to find and explore topics using subject directories, to conduct background research and also more focused searching, and to collaborate and exchange feedback via email and online discussion forums.

Class Activities

Bring to class or post online a thread from a newsgroup discussion. Discuss with your class how such a forum might help students explore topic ideas and share information with other interested individuals.

Computer Activities

1. Demonstrate how to conduct a background search of online dictionaries, encyclopedias, and handbooks.

2. Demonstrate how to use *Google* newsgroups. Encourage students to use such forums to trade ideas and share information.

17.2 Get to know the Internet and the Web

Class Activities

1. Discuss with students the basic idea of the Internet and the types of tools that are available via the Internet. Help them to understand how the Web fits into the larger picture of the Internet and how the Web is structured through hypertext documents linked to one another. Introduce them to a browser and its functions.

2. Discuss copyright information with your students. It is important for students to understand that they need to be as careful and conscientious about citing Web sources as they are about citing any other sources used in their research paper.

3. These two activities may be done online in a discussion forum.

Collaborative Activities

Ask students to write a brief paragraph on their understanding of copyright as it relates to information found on the Internet. Have them share their paragraphs in small groups of three to four students in class or in a chat room.

Computer Activities

1. Using a projector, demonstrate the various kinds of Internet tools that students will be using in their research.

2. Go to the Copyright website at *http://www.benedict.com* and use the site as a springboard for a discussion of copyright issues relevant to student researchers.

3. Initiate an online discussion about copyright issues among students in your class, either via email or in a discussion forum. Ask them to summarize the discussion in a brief paragraph to be emailed to you.

17.3 Search the Internet and the Web

Teaching Suggestions

This section introduces students to the important processes and tools used for locating information on the World Wide Web. Spend time with individual students as they are learning how to search on the Internet. It takes a great deal of practice to narrow a search to make efficient use of search engines. Students need to learn to use keyword searches effectively. They need to discriminate among types of search tools in order to decide which are best for which kinds of searches. They should become familiar with Boolean operators. The best time for students to learn to use these tools is at the point of need—when they are actually trying to locate sources for a current research project. Librarians responsible for library instruction have long known that scavenger hunts and random searches not connected to a particular topic typically do not provide good learning experiences for students.

Class Activities

1. Bring to class overheads that illustrate keyword searches using Internet search tools. Discuss searching with keywords and with Boolean operators.

Computer Activities

1. Using a projector, demonstrate the various search tools described in this section. Encourage students to see for themselves by checking out the sources whose Web addresses are provided in the boxes.

2. Demonstrate the BOOKMARKS or FAVORITES feature of different Web browsers. Show students how to save bookmarks to their own disks for later use.

3. Demonstrate the HISTORY feature of a Web browser. Show students how it can retrace their steps in a given search session. Remind them, though, that the history may disappear when they shut down the browser—unless they have set it to remain for a longer period of time (tools>options).

17.4 Model Searches

Teaching Suggestions

Explore with students the library subscription databases available on your campus. Show them how to search for electronic full-text articles on their topics. You might want to invite a librarian to meet with your class to discuss using these types of databases most productively.

The description of Kaycee's Internet search illustrates some of the roadblocks that students might encounter and provides helpful hints on searching. Have students retrace Kaycee's steps, and mention to them that this is how their own searches will most likely progress—with some successes and some dead ends. Then discuss Internet searching with students. Have they had any of the same experiences as Kaycee did? How might the search tools she used have changed in recent months? Are there other search tools that she might have used? How might the lessons learned from her search be applied to their own research projects?

Computer Novice Notes

Many new research tools are introduced in this chapter. Novice computer users will need extra practice in order to understand and use these tools. If possible, spend some extra time in the computer lab with students and offer additional sessions for novices who need help. It might be a good idea to team up with another teacher so that two instructors are available to help students during a given class period.

Connections

Chapters 17 and 18 work together as a unit. Students need to learn how to find Internet sources and how to evaluate them once they find them.

Answers for Chapter 17 *You Try It* Exercises

For all exercises in this chapter, answers will vary.

CHAPTER 18 / *Evaluating Sources*

MULTIMEDIA FOR CHAPTER 18

Video Tutorials	Sample Documents	Writing Activities
Video 18.1 Chapter Introduction	Flow Chart Process for Choosing Sources	*You Try It* 18.1 Choosing Sources
Video 18.2 Finding a Site's Homepage	Sample Print Source with Annotations	*You Try It* 18.2 Evaluating Print Sources
Video 18.3 Using the Internet to Assess Author Credibility	Guidelines Assessing Print Sources	*You Try It* 18.3 Evaluating Online Sources
Video 18.4 Guidelines for Assessing Print Sources	Sample Website with Annotations	*You Try It* 18.4 Charting Trustworthiness
Video 18.5 Evaluating Online Sources	Sample U.S. Government Website with Annotations	*You Try It* 18.5 Suspicious Sources
Video 18.6 Using Domains and URLs to Assess Internet Sources	Checklist Evaluating Source Information	

Video 18.7 Identifying Sites as Personal Homepages		
Video 18.8 Assessing the Appropriateness of Web Sources		
Video 18.9 Checklist for Evaluating Source Information		
Video 1810 Using Wikipedia Appropriately		
Video 18.11 Following a Student's Evaluation of Web Links		

Chapter Highlights

This chapter takes a close look at source evaluation in an effort to help students choose legitimate sources for their research papers. Evaluating sources has always been a challenging task for students, and the advent of the Internet, with its wide range of available materials, has made this task even more formidable. I provide students with specific strategies designed to help them decide whether a source is worth reading and then, if so, whether that source is worth using in their papers. This chapter also helps students see that, although the principles are the same in evaluating print sources and electronic sources, evaluation criteria may differ. Finally, a model search is included to show how one student evaluated a series of Web links for a research project.

Learning Outcomes

The learning outcomes for Chapter 18 are listed in the following chart, along with the relevant sections of the chapter and exercises that teachers can use to evaluate their students' mastery of the objectives. This chart also appears as a clickable link in the etext.

CHAPTER 18 LEARNING OUTCOMES CHART	
To assess your understanding of the Chapter 18 learning outcomes, work the corresponding You Try It exercises and study the relevant chapter sections.	
18.1 Select credible and authoritative sources based on criteria for relevance and reliability.	*You Try It* 18.1 Choosing Sources *You Try It* 18.2 Evaluating Print Sources *You Try It* 18.3 Evaluating Online Sources *You Try It* 18.4 Charting Trustworthiness
18.2 Evaluate appropriate primary and secondary sources.	*You Try It* 18.5 Suspicious Sources
18.3 Evaluate sources collected online, including from scholarly databases.	Study Chapter 18.3a

18.1 Choose legitimate sources

Teaching Suggestions

Initiate with students a discussion about the different kinds of sources they will encounter during their research and the relative merits of these sources. Students need to approach all the sources they read, both print and Internet, with a critical eye. I suggest a two-step evaluative process in which students first decide whether a source is reliable by assessing its relevance, publisher or sponsor, author, timeliness, and cross references. Once they have established that a source is legitimate, they decide whether it is worth using in their paper by assessing its rhetorical stance, content, and other criteria specific to Internet sources. You will need to work with students on this kind of critical approach until it becomes second nature for them.

Class Activities

1. Discuss the rhetorical stance of sources brought to class by students. Who is the target audience? What is the purpose of the source? Look closely at the content as well. What is the tone of the piece? How is the piece developed and what evidence does it use? Stress that this method of evaluation will help students decide whether a source is useful. This activity may also be done in an online discussion forum or chat room.

2. Put copies of two homepages on overhead transparencies. Choose homepages from two very different websites—one that has a reputable sponsor and one that is questionable. Use the homepages as a springboard for discussing the range of information found on the Web and the need to evaluate each source carefully and critically. This activity may also be done in a computer classroom or online in a discussion forum.

Collaborative Activities

1. Have students bring in copies of sources they have encountered in their own research—either print sources or Internet sources. Divide the students into groups of three or four to discuss these sources' reliability. This activity may also be done in an online discussion forum or chat room.

Computer Activities

1. Put "Assessing a Web Source's Appropriateness" on an overhead transparency, and project it for the class. Provide students with copies of a source to examine. Following the suggestions on the transparency, evaluate the source together.

2. Model for students how to locate a website's homepage by traveling up the URL's directory path (see the TECH HELP box).

3. Model for students how to find out about an author through an Internet search (see the TECH HELP box).

4. Find websites whose publisher or sponsor is ambiguous. Discuss with students who the sponsor might be. Mention to students that it is prudent to be very skeptical about a site's information when the site does not provide information about who the publisher or sponsor is.

5. Find websites whose author or date of posting is ambiguous. Discuss with students how important it is to know something about the author of a site and when it was posted or updated.

6. Ask students to bring to class their answers to Exercise 18.1, in which they were asked to evaluate four websites. Use these answers as a springboard for a class discussion of Internet sources.

18.2 Evaluate print sources

Teaching Suggestions

You will want to be sure that students understand that print sources may not be any more reliable than online sources. They need to use their critical judgments no matter what kind of information they are reading.

18.3 Evaluate online sources

Teaching Suggestions

This section provides guidelines for evaluating online sources. After choosing a timely topic that is under discussion on your campus, guide students through a model search and evaluation. The goal is to show students the range of information a search will uncover and the crucial need to read Internet sources with a critical eye.

Class Activities

If you are teaching in a computer classroom, have groups of two or three students conduct a model search together on a single computer and report back to the class. If you are teaching in a regular classroom, make transparencies of the model Web links by printing the relevant Web pages onto transparency sheets, and project them overhead for class discussion. If you are teaching online, have students post the results of their model searches in a discussion forum or chat room.

Computer Novice Notes

When computer novices first conduct research on the Web, they often are simultaneously overwhelmed and overly impressed by the information they find there. Help students build a healthy skepticism about what they encounter on the Web. This is not to say that a critical eye is not needed for print sources, too. But the Web has introduced an entirely new dimension to the publishing world—anyone can become a Web author. Therefore, the range of material is greater on the Web than in print. Spending time with students as they learn about the Web will pay dividends as they become more discerning consumers of Internet information.

Answers for Chapter 18 *You Try It* Exercises

For all exercises in this chapter, answers will vary.

CHAPTER 19 / *Using Sources and Avoiding Plagiarism*

MULTIMEDIA FOR CHAPTER 19

VIDEO TUTORIALS	SAMPLE DOCUMENTS	WRITING ACTIVITIES
Video 19.1 Chapter Introduction	Guidelines Top Ten Ways to Avoid Plagiarism	*You Try It* 19.1 Understanding Plagiarism
Video 19.2 Avoiding Plagiarism	Example Notes in a Computer File	*You Try It* 19.2 Avoiding Unintentional Plagiarism
	Guidelines Acknowledging Sources	*You Try It* 19.3 Write an ineffective Paraphrase
	Example Page 3 of Immigration Table	*You Try It* 19.4 Effective Paraphrasing
	Example Page 4 of Immigration Table	*You Try It* 19.5 Effective Summarizing
	Example Unintentional Plagiarism	
	Example Plagiarized Text Copied from the Internet	

	Example The Original Text at a Website	
	Guidelines Effective Paraphrasing	
	Example A Summary of Source Material	
	Guidelines Effective Summarizing	
	Guidelines Verbs to Use in Signal Phrases	
	Guidelines Effective Quoting	
	Example Computer Notebook with Direct Quotation	

Chapter Highlights

The ability to use sources accurately and appropriately is an important skill for college students to develop. In this chapter, students learn the differences among quoting, paraphrasing, and summarizing from sources and when to do each in their own writing. They also learn techniques for avoiding plagiarism. Numerous examples, both correct and incorrect, help students understand the distinctions made in this chapter and become responsible in their use of sources in their own writing.

Learning Outcomes

The learning outcomes for Chapter 19 are listed in the following chart, along with the relevant sections of the chapter and exercises that teachers can use to evaluate their students' mastery of the objectives. This chart also appears as a clickable link in the etext.

CHAPTER 19 LEARNING OUTCOMES CHART	
To assess your understanding of the Chapter 19 learning outcomes, work the corresponding You Try It exercises and study the relevant chapter sections.	
19.1 Understand how to use sources responsibly.	Study Chapter 19.1
19.2 Understand what plagiarism is and how to avoid it.	*You Try It* 19.1 Understanding Plagiarism *You Try It* 19.2 Avoiding Unintentional Plagiarism
19.3 Understand how to paraphrase and summarize appropriately.	*You Try It* 19.3 Write an Ineffective Paraphrase *You Try It* 19.4 Effective Paraphrasing *You Try It* 19.5 Effective Summarizing
19.4 Understand how to integrate quotations into your papers.	*You Try It* 19.6 Effective Quoting

ESL Note

Writing from sources can be a real challenge for ESL students, as they may have somewhat limited skills in their second languages. In particular, it may be difficult for them to come up with alternative wording in order to paraphrase and summarize from sources. An online thesaurus may help ESL students build their vocabularies. ESL students with rudimentary language skills may have a hard time avoiding plagiarism; they will need considerable help. It is important to note that our definition of plagiarism in this country is culturally based; not all cultures consider the reuse of another person's words to be unethical. In fact, some cultures consider copying another's words to be a compliment, not a crime. You should discuss these issues carefully with ESL students to be certain that they understand the Western conventions surrounding plagiarism.

19.1 Using sources responsibly

Teaching Suggestions

This chapter begins with a review of the critical reading principles. I suggest that you have students reread the discussion of critical reading in Chapter 2, as well as the sections on effective note taking in Chapter 16. If students fully understand the critical reading and note taking procedures, they will understand what is meant by plagiarism and how to avoid it.

Class Activities

1. Have students read and take notes on an article that you provide. Use their notes as the basis for a class discussion on the difference between paraphrasing and summarizing. In taking notes, did they do one or the other or both? Discuss ways to decide whether to quote, paraphrase, or summarize a source. This activity may be done online in a discussion forum or chat room.

19.2 Reading critically and taking accurate notes

Teaching Suggestions

An important skill that students need to develop is reading critically. As they are reading, they also need to be taking accurate notes. For more information on critical reading, have students review Chapter 2.

19.3 Avoiding plagiarism

Teaching Suggestions

What does and does not constitute plagiarism can be both a point of confusion and potential trouble for many students. This section provides a careful review of plagiarism's various forms. Additionally, several examples illustrate how students can maintain academic integrity and acknowledge sources properly.

Class Activities

1. Bring to class an example to project overhead that illustrates an instance of plagiarism that you encountered—perhaps in a prior class. Use the example as a springboard for a discussion of plagiarism. Ask students whether the example illustrates unintentional or intentional plagiarism. Does that make a difference?

2. Put a copy of your college's plagiarism policy on an overhead projector or online. Such a policy will typically be found in the college's catalog or in a student handbook. Read through the policy statement with the class and discuss its ramifications for students. This activity may also be done in a computer classroom or online in a discussion forum.

3. Discuss with students the appropriate use of information downloaded from a website. Because it is so easy to cut and paste electronic information into a research paper, it is crucial that students understand how to document their sources. You might also discuss the availability and use of the "canned" research papers that can be found on the Internet. This activity may also be done in a computer classroom or online discussion forum.

Connections

Many good articles have been written over the years on the subject of plagiarism. An article that I have found especially helpful is Susan H. McLeod, "Responding to Plagiarism: The Role of the WPA," *Writing Program Administration* 15.3 (1992): 7–16.

19.4 Paraphrasing sources accurately

Teaching Suggestions

Paraphrasing takes practice. The more opportunities you can provide for students to work on this skill, the better. As part of the peer review of a preliminary draft, ask students to compare the specific wording of one paraphrase with that of the original source.

Class Activities

Show students how a signal phrase can be used to introduce a paraphrase and how a paraphrase should be documented. Provide students with a paragraph taken from a source, and have them practice paraphrasing from that paragraph. Use the suggestions in this section to guide this activity. This activity may also be done in a computer classroom.

Collaborative Activities

Put "Guidelines: Effective Paraphrasing" on an overhead transparency or post it online. Have students use these guidelines as they evaluate a peer's rough draft, looking specifically for how effectively the writer has paraphrased sources.

Computer Activities

When they are paraphrasing, have students use an online thesaurus to find synonyms to replace words from the original.

Teaching Suggestions

Because cutting and pasting text from the Internet is so easily done, students sometimes fall into the temptation of doing so with wholesale chunks of text or without properly crediting the source, both of which, of course, constitute plagiarism. Section 20d provides a clear example illustrating to students how to steer clear of this pitfall.

19.5 Summarizing sources briefly

Teaching Suggestions

Like paraphrasing, summarizing takes practice. Provide as many opportunities as possible for students to work on this skill. As part of the peer review of a preliminary draft, ask students to look specifically at the summaries of source information.

Class Activities

Show students how a signal phrase can be used to introduce a summary and how a summary should be documented. Provide students with several paragraphs taken from a source, and have them summarize the paragraphs. Use the suggestions in this section to guide this activity. This activity may also be done in a computer classroom or online.

Collaborative Activities

Display "Guidelines for Effective Summarizing" on an overhead transparency. Have students use these guidelines as they evaluate a peer's rough draft, looking specifically for how effectively the peer has used summaries in his or her research paper.

Computer Activities

Have students use the table feature of their word-processing programs to write a summary of a source they are currently using.

Teaching Suggestions

If summarizing, like paraphrasing, takes practice, so does avoiding plagiarism when doing so. This section discusses how students need to both use their own words to summarize information as well as provide proper documentation to avoid plagiarism. This section provides further practice with this technique.

19.6 Quoting sources sparingly

Teaching Suggestions

Students have difficulty integrating quoted material into their papers. Incorporating direct quotations smoothly, without interrupting the flow of the paper, is especially tricky. To help students learn this skill, provide them with practice exercises in which they are asked to incorporate a quoted sentence into a paragraph. Students can work with each other on drafts, looking specifically for the ways in which quotations have been integrated and suggesting ways in which they could be better integrated.

Class Activities

Show students how a signal phrase can be used to introduce a quotation and how a quotation should be documented. Provide students with a paragraph taken from a source, and have them practice taking direct quotations from that paragraph. Use "Guidelines for Effective Quoting" to guide this activity. This activity may also be done in a computer classroom or online.

Collaborative Activities

Put "Guidelines: Effective Quoting" on an overhead transparency or post online. Have students use these guidelines as they evaluate a peer's rough draft, looking specifically for how effectively the writer has integrated direct quotations.

Connections

See also Margaret Kantz, "Helping Students Use Textual Sources Persuasively," *The Allyn & Bacon Sourcebook for College Writing Teachers*, ed. James C. McDonald (Boston: Allyn & Bacon, 1996).

Teaching Suggestions

Teaching students to quote accurately while giving credit where it is due will go a long way in helping them avoid plagiarism. This section provides techniques for maintaining source integrity when quoting material from a variety of sources.

Answers for Chapter 19 *You Try It* Exercises

For all exercises in this chapter, answers will vary.

CHAPTER 20 / *Writing the Research Paper*

MULTIMEDIA FOR CHAPTER 20

VIDEO TUTORIALS	SAMPLE DOCUMENTS	WRITING ACTIVITIES
Video 20.1 Chapter Introduction	Checklist Revising a Research Paper	*You Try It* 20.1 Practice Writing Introductions
Video 20.2 Writing a Thesis Statement	Guidelines Incorporating Visuals	*You Try It* 20.2 Writing a Research Essay
Video 20.3 Writing with Word Processors	Student Paper Kaycee's Research Paper	
Video 20.4 Balancing Voices in a Research Paper		
Video 20.5 Using the Computer Page-Number Feature		
Video 20.6 Using the Computer Footnote Program		

Video 20.7 Formatting Your Research Paper		

Chapter Highlights

In this chapter, students learn to organize and present their research in a coherent way. They are encouraged to review their rhetorical stance and thesis, decide on a voice and tone, plan a structure, and write a draft of their research paper. Although this process is not markedly different from the writing process described in Part 1 of the etext, the steps are reviewed briefly here. Finally, students are advised to review and revise their draft and follow the formatting conventions appropriate to the discipline. An annotated student research paper, which has been previewed throughout this part of the etext, is included as a model.

Learning Outcomes

The learning outcomes for Chapter 20 are listed in the following chart, along with the relevant sections of the chapter and exercises that teachers can use to evaluate their students' mastery of the objectives. This chart also appears as a clickable link in the etext.

CHAPTER 20 LEARNING OUTCOMES CHART	
To assess your understanding of the Chapter 20 learning outcomes, work the corresponding You Try It exercises and study the relevant chapter sections.	
20.1 Understand how to organize and arrange your research information.	Study Chapter 20.1 and 20.2
20.2 Learn how to write and revise a draft of a research paper.	Study Chapter 20.3 and 20.4 You Try It 20.1 Practice Writing Introductions

	You Try It 20.2 Writing a Research Essay or Report
20.3 Learn how to use footnotes.	Study Chapter 20.5
20.4 Learn how to incorporate visuals into your research paper.	Study Chapter 20.5

20.1 Review your rhetorical stance and thesis

Teaching Suggestions

Before they begin to draft their paper, students need to step back from their research in order to assess where it has taken them. Encourage them to review their rhetorical stance and thesis and decide on a voice and tone.

Class Activities

1. Review the section in Chapter 3 on rhetorical stance. Discuss with students possible audiences for their research papers (in person or online via a discussion forum or chat room). Have them write a brief paragraph describing the rhetorical stance they intend to adopt.

2. Find an informational report and an argumentative research paper, and make an overhead of the first page of each (or post online). Ask students to determine whether each piece is informational or argumentative. Then ask them to identify the thesis statement. Discuss how the thesis statement makes a commitment to the reader that must be fulfilled by the writer. Conduct the discussion in class or online in a discussion forum.

3. Bring in examples of research papers differing in voice and tone (or post online). Use these examples as a springboard for a discussion of voices and tones appropriate for a research paper. Conduct the discussion in class or online in a discussion forum.

Computer Activities

Ask students to include in their electronic research notebook a paragraph describing the rhetorical stance they are adopting for their research paper. If you have a LAN or a Web forum, post these paragraphs for student discussion and feedback.

20.2 Plan a structure

Teaching Suggestions

Many students have their own ad hoc method for composing research papers. Instead of coming up with a plan, they simply string together information found in various sources. Encourage them to develop an organizational plan to guide their drafting. Several suggestions are included in this section of the chapter.

Class Activities

1. Put examples of outlines for research papers from prior classes on overhead transparencies for class discussion (or post online). This activity may also be done in a computer classroom or online.

2. Bring in a research paper (or post online) in which no opposing viewpoints are acknowledged. Ask students to supply the missing counterarguments. Discuss (in person or online) how including and refuting opposing viewpoints can make a piece stronger.

3. Review with your class the information on argumentation found in Chapter 4. Discuss methods of argumentation as well as logical fallacies. Return to this discussion when you are ready to have students review each other's drafts. The discussions may be conducted in person or online.

Collaborative Activities

Have students meet in groups to discuss their planning strategies. Through peer feedback, they can improve their organizational plans and perhaps come up with some new ideas. If you are teaching in an online classroom, create online collaborative groups that meet with each other in a chat room.

Computer Activities

1. Demonstrate how to use COPY and PASTE and CLICK and DRAG to organize and sort information from a research notebook. You may also wish to demonstrate using multiple windows and split screens to copy information from the notebook file to the first draft file.

2. Demonstrate how to use the OUTLINE feature of the word-processing program.

20.3 Write a draft

Teaching Suggestions

Students may need help in deciding on a drafting strategy. Discuss with students the suggested strategies outlined in this section of the chapter. Stress to students that they should begin with a plan but remain flexible, since plans may need to be changed during drafting. Then have students explain the strategy they intend to use. You can meet one-on-one with students before they begin drafting, either in person or in an online chat room, to help them outline the draft.

Class Activities

1. Bring in (or post online) examples of research papers in which materials are combined appropriately and also some papers that could use more work. Students should see numerous models, both good and poor, before they begin drafting.

2. Discuss possible drafting strategies with students.

3. Have students brainstorm possible titles for their work in their research notebooks. Encourage them to be innovative and prolific. This activity can get the juices flowing for the drafting process.

Collaborative Activities

Have students write introductory paragraphs in their research notebooks, using the information in Chapter 5.8 as a guideline. Have students gather in small groups of three or four to share their paragraphs. This can be done in person or online via a chat room.

Computer Activities

Demonstrate how students can employ multiple windows, using their prewriting, notebook, and outline files to build their drafts.

20.4 **Review and revise the draft**

Teaching Suggestions

Students should review and revise their own papers before they review each other's. For help with this process, refer them to the "Checklist: Revising a Research Paper."

Class Activities

1. Project the "Checklist: Revising a Research Paper" overhead, to guide students as they review and revise their own papers.

2. Have students review the information on revision in Chapter 6.2.

Collaborative Activities

Ask students to exchange drafts. Have peer reviewers draw a line in the margin with a pencil or a highlighting pen wherever the author is reflecting, synthesizing, or making inferences based on the evidence. This is a good way of alerting students to drafts that are overly derivative, without enough independent thought from the author. This activity may be done online using a discussion forum or email to exchange drafts. Have students use document comments on their peer's draft.

Computer Activities

1. Demonstrate the page-numbering feature of the word-processing system your class is using. Show students how to incorporate headers with page numbers and how to suppress numbering on the cover page.

2. Have students exchange research paper drafts via the class website. Ask students to comment on each other's drafts, using the DOCUMENT COMMENTS and TRACK CHANGES features of their word-processing program.

20.5 **Follow formatting conventions**

Teaching Suggestions

Some teachers like to assign a standardized format for all their students' papers. Others prefer to allow students to choose the format customarily used in their major discipline. Whatever you decide, make sure students understand the appropriate formatting conventions for the assignment. Stress that formats are conventional, just as clothing selections and table manners are conventional. Students need to pay attention to the conventions appropriate to their disciplines so as not to offend or alienate their readers.

Collaborative Activities

Ask students to exchange their Works Cited pages for peer review. Help them to learn to be extremely careful readers, looking closely for formatting details such as underlining or punctuation. They can exchange documents via email or an online discussion forum or file-sharing space.

Computer Activities

1. Demonstrate the PAGE SETUP feature of the word-processing program used by your class. Also acquaint them with PRINT PREVIEW.

2. Demonstrate the FOOTNOTE feature of the word-processing system your class is using. Show students how they can make use of this feature for content footnotes.

3. Demonstrate the MARGIN feature of the word-processing system your class is using. Show students how to indent for long quotations and how to set tabs for paragraph indentations.

4. Demonstrate other formatting features that students may want to use when revising and polishing their research papers, such as underlining, italics, and boldface.

20.6 **Review annotated research papers**

Teaching Suggestions

Use the models from Chapters 21, 22, and 23, along with others that you have collected from prior classes (with student permission, of course) to discuss what makes an effective research paper. The annotations in the margins of the model papers indicate those features that I found noteworthy. You will probably find others, as will your students. These are not perfect papers, by any means; students should feel free to criticize them. But there is also much to praise. Student models that reflect abilities close to those of your own students will be more helpful than professional models, which may tend to intimidate rather than illustrate.

Class Activities

1. Read through the entire model paper, asking each student to read a paragraph. Then go back and look closely at the annotations. Ask students to comment on any other features that they find noteworthy. Encourage critical reading and a questioning attitude. Bring in other models for students to read and discuss.

2. Construct a grading grid, or criteria sheet, that outlines what you consider to be the essential ingredients of an excellent research paper. Go over the grading grid with your students, explaining the features that you will be explicitly looking for as you grade their work. Allow them to use the grading grid as a revision tool.

Computer Activities

Post on a class website an archive of prior student work so that your current students will have models for their research papers.

Answers for Chapter 20 *You Try It* Exercises

For all exercises in this chapter, answers will vary.

CHAPTER 21 / *MLA Documentation Style*

MULTIMEDIA FOR CHAPTER 21

VIDEO TUTORIALS	SAMPLE DOCUMENTS	WRITING ACTIVITIES
Video 21.1 Chapter Introduction	Guidelines Using the MLA Citation System	*You Try It* 21.1 Incorporating In-Text Citations Using MLA Documentation Style
Video 21.2 Locating Source Information for a Book Citation	Chart A Directory for MLA Style Examples	*You Try It* 21.2 Composing Works Cited Entries using MLA Documentation Style
Video 21.3 Locating Source Information in a Journal	Guidelines Formatting MLA Endnotes and Footnotes	
Video 21.4 Locating Source Information in a Newspaper Citation	Example Locating Source Information in a Book	
Video 21.5 Locating Source Information for an Online Journal Citation	Example Locating Source Information in a Journal	

Video 21.6 Locating Source Information for a Citation of a Full-Text Article	Example Locating Source Information in a Newspaper	
Video 21.7 Kaycee's Research Paper	Example Online Journal Article with Corresponding Print Version	
	Example An Internet Site with Navigation Paths or Search Option	
	Example An Entire Internet Site	
	Example A Report found at PEW Center's Website	
	Example Article in an Online Scholarly Journal	
	Example Full-Text Article	
	Student Paper Kaycee's Research Paper	

Chapter Highlights

This chapter provides students with a comprehensive guide to the latest documentation style of the Modern Language Association, the style most commonly used in English language and literature classes. By studying this chapter, students will learn the basic principles underlying MLA documentation. Do not expect them to memorize the details. Rather, they should use this chapter as a point of reference whenever they are writing a research paper from a discipline that uses the MLA documentation style.

Learning Outcomes

The learning outcomes for Chapter 21 are listed in the following chart, along with the relevant sections of the chapter and exercises that teachers can use to evaluate their students' mastery of the objectives. This chart also appears as a clickable link in the etext.

CHAPTER 21 LEARNING OUTCOMES CHART	
To assess your understanding of the Chapter 21 learning outcomes, work the corresponding *You Try It* exercises and study the relevant chapter sections.	
21.1 Understand the purpose of documentation.	Study Chapter 21.1
21.2 Understand how to integrate sources responsibly.	Study Chapter 21.2 *You Try It* 21.1 Incorporating In-Text Citations Using MLA Documentation Style
21.3 Learn how to document sources using MLA style.	Study Chapter 21.3 and 21.4
21.4 Learn how to create works cited lists in MLA style.	Study Chapter 21.5 and 21.6 *You Try It* 21.2 Composing Works Cited Entries Using MLA Documentation Style

21.1–21.4 Document Using the Modern Language Association (MLA) Style

Teaching Suggestions

Students often wonder how and why documentation conventions developed differently in different disciplines. Although there is no clear-cut answer to this question, it is fair to say that the various systems were developed to help researchers follow the thread, or trail, of previous research on a given topic—research on which their own would be built. Make the analogy between familiar conventions and conventions in the disciplines for documentation of scholarly work. Discuss with students some conventions they are familiar with—conventions of dress, speech, or manners, for example. Why were these conventions developed? What purpose do they serve? What does it mean to violate conventions?

Class Activities

1. Assign each student one type of source (for example, a book with multiple authors). The student's task is to find an example of such a source in the library, bring it to class, describe it to the class, and write the appropriate Works Cited entry on the blackboard or whiteboard.

2. Look closely with your class at the model student paper found in Chapter 6, which uses MLA format. Ask them to point out the main features of the citation form and the Works Cited page.

Collaborative Activities

Bring to class the various style guides mentioned in the introduction to the chapter. Have students meet in groups to evaluate the guides. Put their evaluations on an overhead transparency for class discussion.

21.5 Electronic in Media MLA Style

Teaching Suggestions

Students need to understand and recognize the different types of online sources they are likely to encounter while doing research. Time spend going over the documentation format for electronic media as outlined in this section of the chapter is time well-spent.

Computer Activities

Introduce students to any bibliography programs you have available (e.g., *NoodleBib*). Show them how such programs can convert from one documentation style to another—MLA to APA, for example. Caution them, however, that these programs are not flawless and the finished product still requires careful proofreading for accuracy.

21.6 Review an annotated research paper

Teaching Suggestions

It is very helpful to students to review model papers before they begin writing their own research papers. Use this section of the chapter as an opportunity to look closely at Kaycee's research paper. Discuss it with your class, either in person or in an online discussion forum. Share with students any other research papers using MLA format that you may have available (after having obtained your students' permission to share their work). Have them analyze the documentation format, paying attention to both in-text citations and the works cited lists.

Answers for Chapter 21 *You Try It* Exercises

➲ You Try It 21.1 Incorporating In-Text Citations Using MLA Documentation Style

1. The narrator says, "Although she said nothing I felt guilty and ashamed, as though I had been caught trespassing . . ." (du Maurier, *Rebecca* 90; ch. 9).

2. According to Issel, "There are areas of the country where testing has occurred at a high proportion of regular intervals where the chance of finding a test-positive horse approaches zero," (qtd. in Meszoly 56).

3. A recent *Newsweek* article states that "sea levels will likely rise more than 18 inches in the 21st century" ("Is It Just Us" 10).

4. Kumpf suggests, "We may compare the *first impression* [of a text] to the term 'curb appeal' used by realtors, a term that refers to the feeling prospective buyers have when viewing a house while still in the car parked at the curb, or in some cases in the driveway" (405).

5. According to a recent article, "Computer animation is a brute-force project of converting graphic art into two-dimensional pixels, and, more recently, into three-dimensional polygons, the building blocks of digital pictures" (Seabrook 89).

6. The Plain Language Action Network states that "if you write for the government, chances are you deal with the Office of the Federal Register. The Federal Register now strongly supports plain language" ("Plain Language").

7. "Soseki's works often dwell on the alienation of modern humanity, the search for mortality, and the difficulty of human communication" ("Natsume Soseki").

8. One Web design expert states, "It's difficult to arrange information into categories, hierarchies, and sequences that make sense to users. But it is the single-most important part of developing electronic documents" ("Info.Design").

9. Lyons states, "There is a considerable body of anatomical and physiological evidence to suggest that human beings are designed, as it were, for the production and reception of speech" (*Semantics* 1:87–88), and he also notes, "Attempts have been made . . . to train chimpanzees to use spoken language; and they have met with little success" (*Semantics* 1:97).

10. According to one source, "Motorcyclists have challenged the [helmet] law, but state courts have generally upheld it because it affects the biker's right to receive insurance compensation for injuries" (Savageau and Loftus 16).

◗ *You Try It* 21.2 Composing Works Cited Entries Using MLA Documentation Style

21.2a

1. Du Maurier, Daphne. *Rebecca*. 1938. New York: Avon, 1971. Print.

2. Meszoly, Joanne. "Is a New Strategy Needed to Control EIA?" *Equus*

    Nov. 2206: 54–61. Print.

3. "Is It Just Us, or Is It Hot in Here?" *Newsweek* 6 Nov. 2000: 10. Print.

4. Kumpf, Eric P. "Visual Metadiscourse: Designing the Considerate Text." *Technical Communication Quarterly* 9.4 (2000): 401–24. *Academic Search Premier.* Web. 15 Oct. 2002.

5. Seabrook, John. "Game Master." *New Yorker* 6 Nov. 2006:88–99. Print.

6. Plain Language Action Network. Nov. 2006. Web. 28 Nov. 2006.

7. "Natsume Soseki." *The Columbia Encyclopedia.* 6th ed., 2001. Web. 28 Feb. 2006.

8. Info.Design. 2005. Web. 19 Feb. 2006.

9. Lyons, John. *Semantics.* 2 vols. London: Cambridge UP, 1977. Print.

10. Savageau, David, and Geoffrey Loftus. *Places Rated Almanac.* 6th ed. New York: Macmillan, 1997. Print.

21.1b

1. Fishman, Charles. *The Wal-Mart Effect: How the World's Most Powerful Company Really Works—and How It's Transforming the American Economy.* New York: Penguin, 2006. Print.

2.   United States. Dept. of Health and Human Services. *A Quick Guide to Plague: Prairie Dogs Can Harbor Fleas Infected with Plague Bacteria.* Atlanta: GPO, 2000. Print.

3.   Cervantes Saavedra, Miguel de. *The Ingenious Gentleman Don Quixote de la Mancha.* Trans. J. M. Cohen. Franklin Center, PA: Franklin Library, 1979. Print.

4.   Nabokov, Vladimir. *Lectures on Don Quixote.* Ed. Fredson Bowers. New York: Harcourt, 1983. *Electronic Text Center.* Ed. David Seaman, 2009. Web. 1 Jan. 2010.

5.   Weiner, Eric. "The Real Kazakhstan: What Does Borat Get Right and Wrong about His Native Land?" *Slate.* 3 Nov. 2006. Web. 20 Nov. 2006.

6.   Hartman, C. A., T. M. Manos, C. Winter, D. M. Hartman, B. Li, and J. C. Smith. "Effects of T'ai Chi Training on Function and Quality of Life Indices in Older Adults with Osteoarthritis." *Journal of the American Geriatric Society* 48.12 (2000): 1553–59. Abstract. *PubMed.* Web. 3 Jan. 2007.

7.   Carroll, Lewis. *The Complete Illustrated Works of Lewis Carroll.* Ed. Edward Guiliano. New York: Avenel. Print.

8.   Stahl, Leslie. "Interview of J. K. Rowling." *Sixty Minutes*. CBS. 31

      Dec. 2000. Television.

9.   Phillips, Jim. "Qualifications for Student Interns." Message to the

      author. 15 Dec. 2006. E-mail.

10.   United States. Bureau of Labor Statistics. *Employment and*

      Unemployment among Youth—Summer 2000. 22 Aug. 2000.

      Web. 1 Sept. 2006.

CHAPTER 22 / *APA Documentation Style*

MULTIMEDIA FOR CHAPTER 22

VIDEO TUTORIALS	SAMPLE DOCUMENTS	WRITING ACTIVITIES
Video 22.1 Chapter Introduction	Guidelines Using the APA Citation Style	*You Try It* 22.1 Incorporating In-Text Citations Using APA Documentation Format
Video 22.2 Group's Research Report	Chart A Directory to APA Style	*You Try It* 22.2 Composing References Page Entries Using APA Documentation Format
	Guidelines Using the APA Citation Style	
	Guidelines Formatting an APA Reference List	
	Student Paper Group Research Report	

Learning Outcomes

The learning outcomes for Chapter 22 are listed in the following chart, along with the relevant sections of the chapter and exercises that teachers can use to evaluate their students' mastery of the objectives. This chart also appears as a clickable link in the etext.

CHAPTER 22 LEARNING OUTCOMES CHART	
To assess your understanding of the Chapter 22 learning outcomes, work the corresponding *You Try It* exercises and study the relevant chapter sections.	
22.1 Understand the purpose of documentation.	Study Chapter 22.1
22.2 Understand how to integrate sources responsibly.	Study Chapter 22.2 *You Try It* **22.1** Incorporating In-Text Citations Using APA Documentation Format
22.3 Learn how to document sources using APA style.	Study Chapter 22.3 and 22.4
22.4 Learn how to create a References list in APA style.	Study Chapter 22.5 and 22.6 *You Try It* 22.2 Composing References Page Entries Using APA Documentation Format

22.1–22.4 Document Using the American Psychological Association (APA) Style

Teaching Suggestions

When introducing the APA system, compare it to the MLA system so that students will understand the similarities and differences. The basic principles of the two systems are the same: in-text citations connected to a References (Works Cited) page. Both systems are designed to fairly and accurately reflect the sources used in a research paper and to help the student writer avoid plagiarism. The devil is in the details, however. Point out the differences in the in-text citation form and in the References form. Pay special attention to such elements as underlining, capitalization, and position of date. Students should not be expected to memorize the differences between the two systems—only to be aware that they exist. For their own papers, they can use as a guide the model references for whatever system they are using.

Class Activities

1. Provide students with model citations in MLA format and ask them to convert these citations to APA style. Then ask them to convert from APA format to MLA. Put their responses on the blackboard or whiteboard or an overhead transparency for class discussion.

2. Look closely with your class at the model student synthesis paper found in Chapter 8, which uses APA format. Ask students to point out the main features of the citation form and the References page.

Collaborative Activities

If students are using the APA system, ask them to exchange their References pages for peer review. Have the peer check closely for correct APA format, using the model entries found in the etext. Exchanges can be done via email or a discussion forum

Computer Activities

Demonstrate any bibliography features available on the word processing programs your students are using. Explain the strengths and limitations of such features to the students.

22.5 Electronic Media in APA style

Teaching Suggestions

The section on documenting electronic media in APA style is the most comprehensive to be found in any composition book today. It includes the most up-to-date information on APA citation of electronic media with step-by-step guidance. I would suggest that you spend ample time with your students carefully going over this section of the chapter. Bring to class several examples of different types of electronic sources and practice documenting them together as a class.

22.6 Review an Annotated Research Report

Teaching Suggestions

It is a good idea to spend time with your students going over various models with APA style. It takes time and practice for students to get used to recognizing the various documentation conventions and formats.

Computer Activities

If you have access to a computer classroom, demonstrate for your class Internet sources that they can practice documenting. Students will have the most trouble figuring out what information on the website is relevant to the citation and will need considerable guidance.

Answers for Chapter 22 *You Try It* Exercises

➲ *You Try It* 22.1 Incorporating In-Text Citations Using APA Documentation Format

1. As Sellin and Winters point out, "With the proliferation of email, instant messaging, secure intranets, video conferencing, the ubiquitous fax machine, and the telephone, virtual teaming is on the increase" (2005, p. 3).

2. The Committee on College Composition and Communication Language Statement asserts that "a nation proud of its diverse heritage and its cultural and racial variety will preserve its heritage of dialects" (1974, p. 2).

3. Cole and McLeod state, "This study demonstrated that the selection of the stimulus is exceptionally important in measuring thematic writing ability" (1999, p. 367).

4. The Native American Graves Protection and Repatriation Act, passed by the United States Congress, specifies that "the return of cultural items covered by this Act shall be in consultation with the requesting lineal descendant or tribe or organization to determine the place and manner of delivery of such items" (1990).

5. Farmer et al. believe that "intervention programs need to be designed and implemented for elementary and secondary schools and should aim at increasing positive attitudes toward science careers for women" (1999, p. 777).

6. It is thought that "media attention on the 'village that quit smoking' added incentive, as did Fiji's cultural emphasis on social cohesion" ("The Village that Quit," 1997, p. 20).

7. As stated in a recent study, "Users may already have a simple form of a device model even before they have used the product. . . . A user who buys a new VCR will develop a mental model of this VCR on the basis of the ones he or she already used" (Westendorp et al., 2000, p. 19).

8. Two recent studies (Bouman, 2000; Wright, 2000) have stressed the need to adapt document design to the special needs of older users.

9. A YWCA supervisor states, "The quality of interns has been improving over the past five years" (C. Roberts, personal communication, April 13, 1998).

10. Of the CIA's home page for kids, an agency spokesperson recently explained, "We're not just people in trench coasts," ("Harriet," 2001, p. 14).

➲ *You Try It* 22.2 Composing References Page Entries Using APA Documentation Format

1. Cromer, R. J. (1998). *Abnormal Psychology* (3rd ed.). New York: W.

   H. Freeman and Co.

2. Gerritsen, M., and Verckens, J. P. (2006). Raising students' intercultural awareness and preparing them for intercultural business (communication) by e-mail. *Business Communication Quarterly, 69* (1), 50–59. Retrieved from http://web.lexisnexis.com/universe

3. Senate Hearing on Indian Affairs. (1998). *Native American Graves Protection and Repatriation Act.* Washington, D. C.: GPO.

4. United States Congress. (1998). *Native American Graves Protection and Repatriation Act, 1990.* Retrieved from http://exchanges.state.gov/education/culprop/ 101–601.html

5. Pinkett, R. D. (2002). *Creating community connections: Sociocultural constructionism and an asset-based approach to community technology and community building.* Unpublished doctoral dissertation, MIT Media Laboratory.

6. Henley, N. M., & Kramarae, C. (1994). Gender, power, and miscommmunication. In C. Roman, S. Juhasz, C. Miller (Eds.), *The Women and Language Debate: A Sourcebook* (pp. 383–406). New Brunswick, NJ: Rutgers University Press.

7. Gibson-Davis, C., and Magnuson, K. (2006). Explaining the patterns of child support among low-income noncustodial fathers. Paper presented at the American Economic Association Conference, Boston.

8. The village that quit. (1997, January/February). *Psychology Today*, 20.

9. Ferguson, C. A. & Neath, S. B. (Eds.) (1981). *Language in the USA*. New York: Cambridge University Press.

10. This is something of a trick question; irretrievable communication such as email is not included in APA references.

CHAPTER 23 / *CMS and CSE Documentation Styles*

MULTIMEDIA FOR CHAPTER 23

Video Tutorials	Sample Documents	Writing Activities
Video 23.1 Chapter Introduction	Guidelines Using the CMS Citation System	*You Try It* 23.1 Composing References Page Entries Using CSE Documentation Format
Video 23.2 Research Report	Chart Directory to the CMS System	
	Guidelines Using the CMS Citation Style for Footnotes or Endnotes	
	Chart A Directory to CSE Style	
	Guidelines Formatting a CSE Reference List	
	Student Paper Group Research Report	

Learning Outcomes

The learning outcomes for Chapter 23 are listed in the following chart, along with the relevant sections of the chapter and exercises that teachers can use to evaluate their students' mastery of the objectives. This chart also appears as a clickable link in the etext.

CHAPTER 23 LEARNING OUTCOMES CHART	
To assess your understanding of the Chapter 23 learning outcomes, work the corresponding You Try It exercises and study the relevant chapter sections.	
23.1 Understand the purpose of documentation.	Study Chapter 23.1 and 23.5
23.2 Understand how to integrate sources responsibly.	Study Chapter 23.2 and 23.6
23.3 Learn how to document sources using CMS or CSE style.	Study Chapter 23.4 and 23.7
23.4 Learn how to create a References list in CMA or CSE style.	Study Chapter 23.3 and 23.8 *You Try It* 23.1 Composing References Page Entries Using CSE Documentation Format

23.1–23.2 Document using the Chicago Manual of Style (CMS)

Teaching Suggestions

The *Chicago Manual of Style* is used widely in a number of disciplines other than languages and literature, including business and some of the humanities, such as history. It is the system commonly used in book publishing, too, so students may find it familiar. Although the system includes both footnotes or endnotes and a bibliography, this section concentrates on footnote or endnote form. It would be a good idea to go over with students how the footnote or endnote system differs from the in-text citation system.

Class Activities

Ask students majoring in history, business, communication, or economics to bring to class a journal from one of those fields. As a class, look closely at the articles in the journal, noting the documentation style and comparing it to the CMS system. If there are differences, have students try to determine why these differences might exist.

Collaborative Activities

If students are using the CMS, ask them to exchange their working bibliographies for peer review. Have the peer check closely for correct CMS format, using the model references. This exchange can be done online via email or in a discussion forum or file sharing space.

23.3 Electronic Media in CMS Style

Teaching Suggestions

For those students in your class using the CMS style, have them analyze the citation formats for electronic media and practice formatting them on their working bibliographies.

23.4–23.7 Document using the CSE Style

Teaching Suggestions

The sciences have no one standard style of documentation. One journal often will differ in style from other journals within the same field. However, the variations are relatively minor. If students understand the basic principles of the Council of Science Editors (CSE) system, any variations required for a particular class should be easy enough to attend to. It would be a good idea to discuss the areas in which these variations tend to occur so that students can watch for them.

Class Activities

1. Look closely with your class at the model student paper found at the end of this chapter, which uses the CSE format. Ask them to point out the main features of the citation form and the Reference list.

2. Ask students majoring in science or engineering to bring to class a journal from one of those fields. As a class, look closely at the articles in the journal, noting the documentation style and comparing it to the CSE system. If there are differences, have students try to determine why these differences might exist.

23.8 Electronic Media in CSE Style

Collaborative Activities

If students are using the CSE system, ask them to exchange their Reference lists for peer review. Have the peer check closely for correct CSE format, using the model references found in the etext. This exchange may be done online via email or a discussion forum or file-sharing space.

23.9 Review an Annotated Research Report

Teaching Suggestions

The research report used as a model in this chapter comes from a technical writing course for engineering students. The students worked together to research and write about a real engineering problem involving the water supply to a city. Have the students watch the video and then read and discuss the report. Ask them to pay close attention to the documentation, both in-text and at the end of the report. Students can discuss the report either in person or online.

Answers To *You Try It* Exercise for Chapter 23

➲ *You Try It* 23.1 Composing References Page Entries Using CSE Documentation Format

1. [Anonymous]. Ethics can boost science. Nature 2000; 408:275.

2. Flather CH, Brady SJ, Knowles MS. Wildlife resource trends in the United States: a technical document supporting the 2000 USDA Forest Service RPA assessment. Fort Collins, CO: US Dept. of Agri., Forest Svc., Rocky Mtn. Res. Stn; 1999.

3. McShea WJ, Underwood HB, Rappole JH, editors. The science of overabundance: deer ecology and population management. Washington, D.C.: Smithsonian Inst. Pr; 1997.

4. O'Gara BW, Yoakum JD, editors. Pronghorn management guides: a compendium of biological and management principles and practices to sustain pronghorn populations and habitat from Canada to Mexico. Washington, D.C.: US Dept. of the Interior, Fish and Wildlife Svc; 1993.

5. Phillips RL, Vasil IK, editors. DNA-based markers in plants. Dordrecht: Kluwer Academic; 1994.

6. Johnson GC, Turk JR, O'Brien D, and Aronson E. Occipital condylar dysplasia in two Jacob sheep. Cornell Vet 1994; 84:91–8.

7. Hawk Ridge Nature Reserve. Migration [Internet]. 1999 [cited 2000 Oct 5]. Available from: http://www.hawkridge.org/migrate.htm

8.   Benton MJ. Stems, nodes, crown clades, and rank-free lists: is

     Linnaeus dead? Biol Rev 2000; 75:633–48.

9.   Barrett J. A salmon a day . . . Newsweek 2006 Oct 30:70.

10. [Anonymous]. Equine reproductive research may help people.

     Equus 2006 Nov: 8–9.

SAMPLE SYLLABI

Sample Syllabus #1
A Syllabus Focused on Genres Using *Comp Online*

Week 1

Focus: Rhetorical Situations and Genres

Materials: *Comp Online: Chapter 1* (Saying What You Mean to Say in a Digital World), *Comp Online: Chapter 9.3* or *9.4* (Exploring: Explanatory or Informative Text)

Key Project: Draft Due: Explanatory or Informative Text

Week 2

Focus: Critical Reading and Viewing

Materials: *Comp Online: Chapter 2* (Critical Reading and Viewing)

Key Project: Revision Due: Explanatory or Informative Text

Week 3

Focus: Evaluative Genres

Materials: *Comp Online: Chapter 3* (The Writing Process), *Comp Online: Chapter 8.1* or *8.2* (Evaluating: Review or Response Essay)

Key Project: Draft Due: Review or Response Essay

Week 4

Focus: Revision

Materials: *Comp Online: Chapter 6* (Rewriting)

Key Project: Revision Due: Review or Response Essay

Week 5

Focus: Reflective Genres

Materials: *Comp Online: Chapter 7.2* (Reflecting: Memoir)

Key Project: Draft Due: Memoir

Week 6

Focus: Memoirs

Materials: Memoirs in Process—Peer Review

Key Project: Revision Due: Memoir

Week 7

Focus: Profiles

Materials: *Comp Online: Chapter 7.3* (Reflecting: Profile)

Key Project: Draft Due: Profile Essay

Week 8

Focus: Structuring Paragraphs

Materials: *Comp Online: Chapter 5* (Structuring Paragraphs)

Key Project: Revision Due: Profile Essay

Week 9

Focus: Academic Genres: Arguing a Position

Materials: *Comp Online: Chapter 4* (Formulating Arguments), *Comp Online: Chapter 10.1* (Arguing a Position)

Key Project: Due: Project Description Memo Arguing for a Research Report or Critical Analysis

Week 10

Focus: Academic Genres: Critical Analysis or Research Report

Materials: *Comp Online: Chapter 16* (The Research Project), *Comp Online: Chapter 10.3* or *10.4* (Critical Analysis Essay or Research Report)

Key Project: Due: Working Bibliography for Critical Analysis or Research Report

Week 11

Focus: The Research Process

Materials: *Comp Online: Chapter 17* (Using the Internet for Research), *Comp Online: Chapter 18* (Evaluating Sources)

Key Project: Due: Thesis Statement and Detailed Outline for Critical Analysis or Research Report

Week 12

Focus: Using Sources Appropriately

Materials: *Comp Online: Chapter 19* (Using Sources and Avoiding Plagiarism)

Key Project: Draft Due: Critical Analysis or Research Report

Week 13

Focus: Writing, Documenting, and Revising the Critical Essay or Research Report

Materials: *Comp Online: Chapter 20* (Writing the Research Paper), *Comp Online: Chapter 21, 22,* or *23* as appropriate for discipline.

Key Project: Due: Thesis Statement and Annotated Bibliography

Week 14

Focus: Exploratory Genres

Materials: *Comp Online: Chapter 9.1* or *9.2* (Exploring: Observation or Ethnography)

Key Project: Draft Due: Observation Essay or Ethnography *PowerPoint* Presentation

Week 15

Focus: Observation or Ethnography

Key Project: Revision Due: Observation Essay or Ethnography *PowerPoint* with Oral Presentation

Sample Syllabus #2
A Syllabus Focused on Argument Using *Comp Online*

Week 1

Focus: Rhetorical situations and genres

Materials: *Comp Online: Chapter 1* (Saying What You Mean to Say in a Digital World), *Comp Online: Chapter 10.1* (Arguing a Position)

Key Project: Draft Due: Position Argument

Week 2

Focus: Critical Reading and Viewing

Materials: *Comp Online: Chapter 2* (Critical Reading and Viewing)

Key Project: Revision Due: Position Argument

Week 3

Focus: Formulating Arguments

Materials: *Comp Online: Chapter 4* (Formulating Arguments), *Comp Online: Chapter 10.2* (Arguing for Change)

Key Project: Draft Due: Change Argument

Week 4

Focus: The Writing Process

Materials: *Comp Online: Chapter 3* (The Writing Process), *Comp Online: Chapter 6.5* (Give and Receive Feedback)

Key Project: Due: Change Argument Peer Reviews

Week 5

Focus: Structuring paragraphs and argument

Materials: *Comp Online: Chapter 5* (Structuring Paragraphs)

Key Project: Revision Due: Change Argument Rewrites

Week 6

Focus: Revision

Materials: *Comp Online: Chapter 6* (Rewriting)

Key Project: Final Draft Due: Change Argument

Week 7

Focus: Arguments in Other Disciplines

Materials: *Comp Online: Chapter 10.3* (Arguing: Critical Analysis Essay)

Key Project: Critical Analysis Essay

Week 8

Focus: Key Features of a Critical Analysis

Materials: *Comp Online: Chapter 10.3a* (Key Features of a Critical Analysis)

Key Project: Draft Due: Critical Analysis Essay

Week 9

Focus: Revising

Materials: Project in Process, Critical Analysis Essay

Key Project: Revision Due: Critical Analysis Essay

Week 10

Focus: Academic Genres: Research Report

Materials: *Comp Online: Chapter 16* (The Research Project), *Comp Online: Chapter 10.4* (Arguing: Research Report)

Key Project: Due: Working Bibliography for Research Report

Week 11

Focus: The Research Process

Materials: *Comp Online: Chapter 17* (Using the Internet for Research), *Comp Online: Chapter 18* (Evaluating Sources)

Key Project: Due: Thesis Statement and Detailed Outline for Research Report

Week 12

Focus: Using Sources Appropriately

Materials: *Comp Online: Chapter 19* (Using Sources and Avoiding Plagiarism)

Key Project: Draft Due: Research Report

Week 13

Focus: Proposals

Materials: *Comp Online: Chapter 10.5* (Proposal)

Key Project: Due: Find an RFP and analyze it

Week 14

Focus: Proposals and Presentations

Materials: *Comp Online: Chapter 10.5a* (Key Features of a Proposal)

Key Project: Due: PowerPoint Presentation of Proposal Plan

Week 15

Focus: Proposals

Materials: *Comp Online: Chapter 10.5b* (A Brief Guide to Writing a Proposal)

Key Project: Due: Proposal

Sample Syllabus #3
A Syllabus Focused on Digital Media Using *Comp Online*

Week 1

Focus: Rhetorical Situations and Genres

Materials: *Comp Online: Chapter 1* (Saying What You Mean to Say in a Digital World), *Comp Online: Chapter 8.1* (Review essay)

Key Project: Due (in-class writing): Review of a Viral Video

Week 2

Focus: Critical Reading and Viewing

Materials: *Comp Online: Chapter 2* (Critical Reading and Viewing), *Comp Online: Chapter 8.3* (Interpretive Essay)

Key Project: Due: Interpretation of a Song or CD

Week 3

Focus: Online Journals

Materials: *Comp Online: Chapter 7.5* (Reflecting: Blog)

Key Project: Draft Due: Personal Blogsite with Journal Entry

Week 4

Focus: Auditory Literacy

Materials: *Comp Online: Chapter 7.1* (Reflecting: Story)

Key Project: Revision Due: Personal Blogsite Including a Story

Week 5

Focus: Argument and Proposals

Materials: *Comp Online: Chapter 4* (Formulating Arguments), *Comp Online: Chapter 10.5* (Arguing: Proposals)

Key Project: Due: Topic Proposals for Audio Research Report (podcast)

Week 6

Focus: Research

Materials: *Comp Online: Chapter 16* (The Research Project)

Key Project: Due: Working Bibliography for Audio Research Report

Week 7

Focus: Audio Research Report (podcast)

Materials: *Comp Online: Chapter 10.4* (Arguing: Research Report), *Comp Online: Chapter 17* (Using the Internet for Research)

Key Project: Audio Research Report in Process

Week 8

Focus: Audio Research Report (podcast)

Materials: *Comp Online: Chapter 18* (Evaluating Sources)

Key Project: Audio Research Report Outline or Storyboard

Week 9

Focus: Audio Research Report (podcast)

Materials: *Comp Online: Chapter 19* (Using Sources and Avoiding Plagiarism)

Key Project: Draft Due: Audio Research Report

Week 10

Focus: Visual Rhetoric

Materials: *Comp Online: Chapter 2.3* (Engage Actively and Critically in the Viewing Process), *Comp Online: Chapter 8.1* (Evaluating: Review Essay)

Key Project: Draft Due: Photo Review Essay

Week 11

Focus: Revision

Materials: *Comp Online: Chapter 6* (Rewriting)

Key Project: Revision Due: Photo Review Essay

Week 12

Focus: Digital Videos

Materials: *Comp Online: Chapter 7.4* (Reflecting: Montage)

Key Project: Topic Proposals for Video Montage

Week 13

Focus: Digital Videos

Materials: Video Montage in Process

Key Project: Draft Due: Video Montage

Week 14

Focus: Revision and Portfolios

Materials: Media Projects in Process

Key Project: Media Projects in Process

Week 15

Focus: Portfolios

Key Project: Due: Portfolio with Revised Media Projects (Blogsite, Audio Research Report Podcast, Photo Review Essay, Video Montage)

Sample Syllabus #4
A Syllabus Focused on Art and Humanities Using *Comp Online*

Week 1

Focus: Rhetorical situations and genre

Materials: *Comp Online: Chapter 1* (Saying What You Mean to Say in a Digital World), *Comp Online: Chapter 7.1* (Reflecting: Story)

Key Project: Draft Due: Short Nonfiction Story

Week 2

Focus: Critical Reading and Viewing

Materials: *Comp Online: Chapter 2* (Critical Reading and Viewing)

Key Project: Revision Due: Short Nonfiction Story

Week 3

Focus: Response Essays

Materials: *Comp Online: Chapter 3* (The Writing Process), *Comp Online: Chapter 8.2* (Evaluating: Response Essay)

Key Project: Draft Due: Response Essay

Week 4

Focus: Interpreting Literature

Materials: *Comp Online: Chapter 4* (Formulating Arguments), *Comp Online: Chapter 8.3* (Evaluating: Interpretive Essay)

Key Project: Interpretive Essay

Week 5

Focus: Interpreting Literature

Materials: *Comp Online: Chapter 5* (Structuring Paragraphs)

Key Project: Draft Due: Interpretive Essay

Week 6

Focus: Revision

Materials: *Comp Online: Chapter 6* (Rewriting)

Key Project: Revision Due: Interpretive Essay

Week 7

Focus: Analyzing Art

Materials: *Comp Online: Chapter 10.3a* (Critical Analysis Essay--Key Features)

Key Project: Critical Analysis of a Painting or Photograph

Week 8

Focus: Photographs and Paintings

Materials: *Comp Online: Chapter 2.3* (Engage Actively and Critically in the Viewing Process)

Key Project: Draft Due: Critical Analysis of a Painting or Photograph

Week 9

Focus: Photographs and Paintings

Materials: *Comp Online: Chapter 10.3b* (Critical Analysis Essay--Brief Guide)

Key Project: Revision Due: Critical Analysis of a Painting or Photograph

Week 10

Focus: Writing About People

Materials: *Comp Online: Chapter 7.3a* (Profile Essays, Key Features)

Key Project: Profile

Week 11

Focus: Writing About People

Materials: *Comp Online: Chapter 7.3b* (Profile Essays, Brief Guide)

Key Project: Draft Due: Profile Essay

Week 12

Focus: Profiles

Materials: Profiles in Process

Key Project: Revision Due: Profile Essay

Week 13

Focus: Music and Film

Materials: *Comp Online: Chapter 8.1* (Evaluating: Review Essay)

Key Project: Review Essay

Week 14

Focus: Reviews

Materials: Reviews in Process

Key Project: Draft Due: Review Essay

Week 15

Focus: Reviews

Key Project: Revision Due: Review Essay

Sample Syllabus #5
A Syllabus Focused on Modes Using *Comp Online*

Week 1

Focus: Rhetorical Situations and Genres

Materials: *Comp Online: Chapter 1* (Saying What You Mean to Say in a Digital World), *Comp Online: Chapter 5.2* (Write Coherence Paragraphs with Clear Patterns of Organization)

Key Project: Practice Writing Paragraphs—*You Try Its* in Chapter 5

Week 2

Focus: Reflecting and Personal Genres

Materials: *Comp Online: Chapter 3* (The Writing Process), *Comp Online: Chapter 7* (Reflecting)

Key Project: Draft Due: Memoir or Story

Week 3

Focus: Revision

Materials: *Comp Online: Chapter 6* (Rewriting)

Key Project: Revision Due: Memoir or Story

Week 4

Focus: Description and Profiles

Materials: *Comp Online: Chapter 7.3* (Reflecting: Profile Essay)

Key Project: Draft Due: Profile

Week 5

Focus: Revising Profiles and Using Visuals

Materials: *Comp Online: Chapter 4.11* (Visual Argument)

Key Project: Revision Due: Profile

Week 6

Focus: Evaluating and Reviews

Materials: *Comp Online: Chapter 8.1* (Evaluating: Review Essay), *Comp Online: Chapter 2.3* (Engage Actively and Critically in the Viewing Process)

Key Project: Draft Due: Review

Week 7

Focus: Evaluating and Reviews

Materials: *Comp Online: Chapter 2* (Critical Reading and Viewing)

Key Project: Revision Due: Review

Week 8

Focus: Exploring and Comparisons and Contrasts

Materials: *Comp Online: Chapter 9.1* (Exploring: Observation)

Key Project: Draft Due: Comparison or Contrast Observation Essay

Week 9

Focus: Exploring and Problem and Solution

Materials: *Comp Online: Chapter 9.4* (Exploring: Informative Texts)

Key Project: Revision Due: Comparison or Contrast Observation Essay

Week 10

Focus: Arguing

Materials: *Comp Online: Chapter 10.1* (Arguing a Position)

Key Project: Due: Memo Outlining Position Argument

Week 11

Focus: Arguing

Materials: *Comp Online: Chapter 4* (Formulating Arguments)

Key Project: Draft Due: Position Argument

Week 12

Focus: Arguing

Materials: Position Argument in Process

Key Project: Revision Due: Position Argument

Week 13

Focus: Critical Analysis or Research Report

Materials: *Comp Online: Chapter 16* (The Research Project), *Comp Online: Chapter 17* (Using the Internet for Research), *Comp Online: Chapter 10.3* or *10.4* (Arguing: Critical Analysis Essay or Research Report)

Key Project: Due: Working Bibliography for Critical Analysis or Research Report

Week 14

Focus: Using Sources Appropriately

Materials: *Comp Online: Chapter 18* (Evaluating Sources), *Comp Online: Chapter 19* (Using Sources and Avoiding Plagiarism)

Key Project: Draft Due: Critical Analysis or Research Report

Week 15

Focus: Writing, Documenting, and Revising the Critical Essay or Research Report

Materials: *Comp Online: Chapter 20* (Writing the Research Paper), *Comp Online: Chapter 21, 22,* or *23* as appropriate for discipline.

Key Project: Revision Due: Critical Analysis or Research Report